WARRIOR • 151

SAMURAI WOMEN
1184–1877

STEPHEN TURNBULL   ILLUSTRATED BY GIUSEPPE RAVA

Series editor Marcus Cowper

OSPREY PUBLISHING
Bloomsbury Publishing Plc

Kemp House, Chawley Park, Oxford OX2 9PH, UK
1385 Broadway, 5th Floor, New York, NY 10018, USA
29 Earlsfort Terrace, Dublin 2, Ireland
Email: info@ospreypublishing.com
www.ospreypublishing.com

OSPREY is a trademark of Osprey Publishing, a division of
Bloomsbury Publishing Plc

First published in Great Britain in 2010

A CIP catalogue record for this book is available from the
British Library.

Print ISBN: 978 1 84603 951 5
ePub: 978 1 78096 333 4
ePDF: 978 1 84603 952 2

Editorial by Ilios Publishing Ltd, Oxford, UK
   (www.iliospublishing.com)
Page layout by Mark Holt
Index by Alison Worthington
Typeset in Sabon and Myriad Pro
Originated by PPS Grasmere
Printed and bound in India by Replika Press Private Ltd.

22 23 24 25 26 15 14 13 12 11 10

Dedication
To Wynzie and Mair Richards, with thanks for years of
friendship and support.

Editor's note
Unless otherwise indicated, all images in this book are the
propertyof the author.

Artist's note
Readers may care to note that the original paintings from which
the colour plates in this book were prepared are available for
private sale. The Publishers retain all reproduction copyright
whatsoever. All enquiries should be addressed to Giuseppe Rava
via the following website:

www.g-rava.it

The Publishers regret that they can enter into no
correspondence upon this matter.

The Woodland Trust
Osprey Publishing supports the Woodland Trust, the UK's
leading woodland conservation charity.

www.ospreypublishing.com
To find out more about our authors and books visit our
website. Here you will find extracts, author interviews,
details of forthcoming events and the option to sign-up
for our newsletter.

CONTENTS

SAMURAI WOMEN 1184–1877

INTRODUCTION: THE ELUSIVE SAMURAI WOMAN

The lives and exploits of the samurai warriors of Japan are among the best-recorded accounts of fighting men anywhere in the world. Chronicles, diaries and *gunkimono* (epic war stories) abound, relating in immense detail both their individual prowess and their contribution to the development of military technology in medieval and early modern Japan. Yet to a very large extent these eyewitness accounts, stories and legends about the samurai are an all-male affair, making the female samurai warrior a very elusive creature. The woman's role seems to be exercised only behind the scenes: in palaces, council chambers and living quarters where decisions were made, alliances arranged and intrigues unfolded. In those situations the influence of women, both directly and indirectly, has long been recognized to have been considerable, because, as wives, daughters and mothers, the women of the samurai class could exert a huge influence over the political process. In their less welcome roles as pawns in the marriage game, negotiators or go-betweens, women also played a vital and hazardous part in the drama of medieval Japan. The samurai woman as a fighting warrior, by contrast, appears to be almost non-existent.

However, even though authentic accounts of fighting women are relatively rare when compared with the immense amount of material on male warriors, they exist in sufficient numbers to allow us to regard the exploits of female warriors as the greatest untold story in samurai history. Over a period of eight centuries female samurai warriors are to be found on battlefields, warships and the walls of defended castles. Their family backgrounds range across all social classes from noblewomen to peasant farmers. Some were motivated by religious belief, others by politics, but all fought beside their menfolk with a determination and bravery that belied their gender, and, when the ultimate sacrifice was called for, they went willingly to their deaths as bravely as any male samurai. Some women achieved fame by employing their skills in the martial arts to seek revenge for a murdered relative; others sought mere survival and, when combined with the exploits of women whose role in warfare was of a more indirect nature, the female contribution to samurai history is revealed to be considerable.

The written evidence for samurai women being involved in actual fighting covers two different situations. The first was that of a defended castle where the commander was absent and the responsibility for defence had to be assumed by his wife. In nearly all such cases the castellans' wives' roles

With the destruction of his brother, Minamoto Yoritomo's newly established shogunate appeared unassailable, but when Yoritomo died in 1199 from a riding accident the Minamoto power began to decline, and following the seemingly all-male triumph of the Gempei Wars a woman became the real power behind the throne. Yoritomo had married Hojo Masako (1157–1225), a woman who was remarkably strong-minded. Being intended by her father for someone else, Masako would have no one but Yoritomo, and when her father Hojo Tokimasa locked her away she escaped and stayed with the future shogun for the rest of his life. Masako entered the religious life on widowhood, but this did nothing to diminish her power, as is indicated by the title by which she is known: the 'nun shogun'. Masako deprived her son Yoriie (1182–1204), the second Minamoto shogun, of absolute power, and set up instead a ruling council with Hojo family members in high places. When an uprising began in the name of the rightful shogun the Hojo defeated the insurgents and had Yoriie assassinated.

Power remained in Masako's hands when Yoriie's son Kugyo (1201–1219) was passed over in succession and her second son Sanetomo (1192–1219) became the third, and last, Minamoto shogun. He was only 12 years old, and a year later his grandfather turned against him, proposing his own son-in-law as an alternative candidate for shogun. But the plot was revealed to Masako, and, such was her hold on *bakufu* affairs that she succeeded in having the pretender shogun murdered and her father packed off to a monastery. But poor Sanetomo enjoyed for only a few years the dignity of shogun. In 1219 he was assassinated within the precincts of the Tsurugaoka Hachiman Shrine

BELOW LEFT
Dressed in their late husbands' suits of armour, Wakazakura and Kaede visited their sorrowing mother-in-law to console her. This hanging scroll is in the museum of the Ioji Temple in Iizaka, where the Sato brothers are buried.

BELOW
A livelier version of the legend of the Sato wives has them taking part in actual fighting rather than merely dressing up in their husbands' armour, as illustrated by this print.

in Kamakura. The murderer was his nephew the aggrieved Kugyo, and when he was killed in revenge the line of the Minamoto died out, leaving Masako's relatives free to become rulers of Japan. They are known as the Hojo *shikken* (regency), because their lack of descent from the Minamoto family would not permit them to take the title of shogun. In this capacity the Hojo ruled Japan until their destruction in 1333.

The 'nun shogun' may never have wielded a sword in anger, but the early years of the Minamoto shogunate also witnessed a little-known rebellion in which a female samurai warrior took part. The incident is called the Kennin Rebellion from the *nengu* (year period) of Kennin (1201–03) in which it began. It was led by the Jo family who were descended from Taira stock and lived in Echigo Province in north central Japan. Jo Sukenaga was defeated and killed by Minamoto Yoshinaka in 1182, after which his brother Nagamochi was pardoned by Yoritomo and served the new shogun in his campaign against the Oshu-Fujiwara in 1189. He then revolted against the shogunate along with his nephew Sukemori and his sister Hangaku Gozen, who is also known as Itagaki Gozen. Jo Sukemori controlled the castle of Torisaka, and it was there that Hangaku Gozen became the first in an honourable line of samurai women to defend a castle. Fortresses during the 13th century were little more than elaborate wooden stockades, but Hangaku Gozen is credited with defending it for three months against Sasaki Moritsuna's *bakufu* army. She led and inspired the garrison from the top of a tower, and Hangaku's army surrendered only when an arrow wounded her. The chronicle *Azuma Kagami* (*The Mirror of the East*) relates how she was captured, taken to Kamakura, the shogun's capital, and presented to the shogun Minamoto Yoriie. Her fate should have been to commit *seppuku* (ritual suicide), but, the entry for the 28th day of the 6th month reveals a happy ending because several of Yoriie's leading warriors were very taken with her bravery and her example. One, named Asari Yoshito went further and proposed that he and Hangaku should marry. The shogun agreed, and the couple married and eventually produced a son. Murdoch, in his *History of Japan*, quotes an unknown source that Asari married her 'in spite of her ugliness' and 'on account of her great courage'.

The triumphant Hojo *shikken* faced its greatest challenge when Mongol armies under Kublai Khan invaded Japan in 1274. Women were among the numerous victims of the attacks on the islands of Tsushima and Iki that

A **HANGAKU GOZEN RIDES INTO BATTLE AT THE SIEGE OF TORISAKA CASTLE, 1201**

Although much less well known than her near contemporary Tomoe Gozen, Hangaku Gozen was a skilled female samurai warrior of the early Kamakura period. She assisted her nephew in the defence of the castle of Torisaka in 1201. Here we see her taking part in a dramatic charge out of the fortified gate of Torisaka. While archers keep up covering fire from the tower above the gate, Hangaku Gozen rides into action swinging her *naginata*, the traditional weapon of the female warrior. Hangaku was admired more for her bravery than her beauty, so she is shown here as a plain-looking woman, although she has dispensed with a helmet to allow her features to inspire her followers. She is wearing an elaborate *yoroi* armour, the choice of generals. It is laced with red silken cords, and the scales are embellished with delicate gilded features. One arm has been left free of armour to allow an easier drawing of the bow. Her bow has been left behind, but she still has a quiver at her belt and a spare bowstring reel hanging from her scabbard. The men with her are typical rough samurai warriors of the age, armed like her with *naginata* or with swords. Their suits of armour are much simpler in design. The fortified gateway is based on the reconstructed example at the Fujiwara Heritage Village near Ichinoseki, while Hangaku Gozen's appearance is taken from a woodblock print by Yoshitoshi.

During the invasion of Iki by the Mongols the women of the island were rounded up and tied together with cords passed through their pierced hands. They were then used as a human shield when the invading army approached Hinotsume Castle. When the victorious fleet sailed for Kyushu the survivors of this treatment were strung along the gunwales of the ships. This painting of the incident hangs in the Mongol Invasion Memorial Museum in Hakata.

the Mongols captured prior to assaulting the mainland. Tsushima was quickly overrun, and the defenders of Iki, overwhelmed by the armed landing, retreated to the island's strongpoint – the stockade fortress of Hinotsume commanded by the island's governor Taira Kagetaka. Before the Mongols' final assault Kagetaka ordered one of his samurai to take his daughter Katsurahime to safety. They were to proceed by boat to Dazaifu, the regional headquarters on Kyushu to advise the government about the situation. The account tells us that Katsurahime's maid, dressed in armour as a gesture of defiance, went with her to the beach to bid her farewell and then returned to fight. By the time Katsurahime's boat reached the open sea the Mongol fleet had appeared in the bay on that side of the island and she was killed by arrow fire.

One grisly detail concerning Iki that is reported in more than one account is that the Mongols rounded up the women of the island and tied them together with cords passed through their pierced hands. They were then used as a human shield as the army approached Hinotsume Castle. When the victorious fleet then sailed for Kyushu the survivors of this treatment were strung along the gunwales of the ships.

The 14th century in Japan was marked by the Nambokucho Wars, a long series of conflicts originating from an attempt by Emperor Go-Daigo to re-assert the ancient imperial power. His supporters first overthrew the Hojo Regency, only to divide into two camps when rewards were not as generous as they had hoped. One faction, of Minamoto descent, set up a new shogunate under the Ashikaga name and went to war against the imperialists. Copious historical records and one famous *gunkimono*, the *Taiheiki*, contain many references to women as victims of war, most notably during the fall of Kamakura in 1333. The battle for the Hojo's capital was fierce and ended with the last leaders of the Hojo *shikken* committing mass suicide. Much street fighting took place and many women were slaughtered. It is likely that the number killed at Kamakura was high because the layout of the city, with mountains on three sides and the sea on the other, did not permit the usual practice of women and children fleeing for safety to neighbouring hills and forests. This did not always guarantee a refuge, because a document from 1337 implies that the women and children who fled a different conflict in this way met their ends in the mountains and forests.

The *Taiheiki*'s long account of the fall of Kamakura includes the sad story of the samurai Moritaka who is sent to the wife of his leader to take away their son. The intention was that his own father should kill him rather than let him suffer the disgrace of being captured by the enemy. In great sorrow his mother agrees, and takes the son from his ladies-in-waiting: 'Heedless of men's eyes, the weeping nurse called Osai ran after him barefooted for 500 or 600 yards, falling down on to the ground again and again, until resolutely he caused his horse to run, that she might not find him out. And when her eyes beheld him no longer, the nurse Osai cast her body into a deep well and perished.'

The nature of the Nambokucho Wars allowed many small-scale skirmishes to take place where the military objectives were localized, and in these accounts we can identify some interesting observations about women fighting. One document dated 23 December 1329 notes briefly that a battle was fought at a place called Oishi no sho between a samurai and his divorced wife! An unusual example of the status a woman could enjoy is provided by the 1337 document cited above that includes a number of petitions for reward from warriors who have distinguished themselves in various battles. The list is validated by a woman's signature.

Women in the Age of Warring States
The Ashikaga shoguns ruled Japan for over two centuries, although the great convulsion of the Onin War from 1467 to 1477 severely curtailed their centralizing influence. The Onin War led to the time known as the *Sengoku Jidai* or 'Age of Warring States', where local *daimyo* took charge of their own affairs and fought one another for territory. It took a century of conflict before Japan was once again unified, and the intervening years provided many an opportunity for women to appear on the field of battle. One example is Ichikawa Tsubone, the wife of a retainer of the Mori family of western Japan. When her husband was absent on campaign she assumed responsibility for the defence of the castle of Mushiro. The Shimazu family of southern Kyushu are recorded as having used women as spies, and one woman servant who pretended that she been ignominiously dismissed by the Shimazu was given refuge by their enemies only to spread false information about the Shimazu's defences.

Attacks on *yamashiro* (mountain-top castles), the characteristic *daimyo*'s fortress, provided many unwelcome opportunities for women to be involved in the defence and to suffer the ultimate sacrifice if the castle fell. Suicide within a burning castle may have been the ultimate act of loyalty for a woman of the samurai class, but more mundane duties could be required of her during her lifetime. Her husband would be the follower of a *daimyo*, whose fields he would till or at the very least manage, and in whose army he would fight. Towards the end of the Sengoku Period the latter military function

In this section from a painted scroll of the 'Later Three Years War' we see several captives including women, being led away by the victorious army. This is taken from a reproduction of the original scroll that is owned by the Memorial Museum at Gosannen in Akita Prefecture.

The relative status between a high-ranking samurai and his wife is beautifully illustrated in this display at the Fujiwara Heritage Village near Ichinoseki. Fujiwara Kiyohira is seated here in his living quarters accompanied by his wife.

became the sole duty for a samurai, but throughout this time of war samurai had to accept that all the members of their families were there in the service of their lords, so there were many occasions when women had to provide necessary back-up for their menfolk. In the case of the wives of lower-ranking samurai this might simply take the form of labouring jobs. Hojo Ujikuni's orders of 1587 for the maintenance of the walls of Hachigata Castle required his followers to make repairs after typhoon damage in preference to mending their own homes, and that if they were away on campaign the work had to be done by their wives and maidservants.

Even if they were not killed the fate of the womenfolk of a defeated army could be a savage one. Rape is recorded throughout samurai history. In *Mutsuwaki,* the history of the so-called Former Nine Years War that was fought from 1055 to 1062, it states: 'Within the fortress dozens of beautiful women coughed in the smoke and sobbed miserably, all dressed in damask, gauze and green stuff shot with gold. Every last one of them was dragged out and given to the warriors.'

When Minamoto Yoshinaka's forces entered Kyoto in 1183 one of his samurai, named in the *Gempei Josuiki* as Higuchi Kanemitsu, captured some high-ranking women and for five or six days 'exposed them to shame' – a euphemism for rape. The women threatened either to kill themselves or become nuns if Kanemitsu was not punished, and he was put to death. In *Bushido: the Soul of Japan* Nitobe gives the example of an unnamed young woman who, having been taken prisoner, seeing herself in danger of violence at the hands of the samurai, says that she will submit to their pleasure, provided that she is first allowed to write a letter to her sisters, whom war had scattered in every direction. When the letter is finished she runs off to the nearest well and saves her honour by drowning herself. The soldiers find the letter and discover that she has composed a farewell poem as noble as any from the brush of a departing samurai:

> For fear lest clouds may dim her light
> Should she but graze this nether sphere
> The young moon poised above the height
> Doth hastily betake to flight.

The women of the *ikki*

During the early Sengoku Period one of the only alternatives to serving a *daimyo* was to become a member of a self-governing *ikki* or league. The members of an *ikki* were often at odds with the local *daimyo* who was endeavouring to build his own retainer base where loyalty was paid solely to him. In the extreme case of Kaga Province the local *ikki* ousted their *daimyo* and ruled the province themselves until being overcome by the superior military force of Oda Nobunaga (1534–82), the first of Japan's unifiers.

Oda Nobunaga was the sworn enemy of the 'people power' expressed by an *ikki*, and from 1570 to 1580 conducted a savage war against the most famous *ikki* of all: the Ikko-*ikki*, the armies fielded by the communities who followed Jodo-Shinshu (the True Pure Land Sect), whose fortified temples and towns housed communities to whom the practice of their religion was a fundamental part of life. Jodo-Shinshu's Ikko-*ikki* armies threatened a growing *daimyo* both militarily and economically, and Oda Nobunaga's ten-year-long intermittent siege of their headquarters, the Ishiyama Honganji (built where Osaka Castle now stands), was destined to be the longest campaign in Japanese history. Just as every member of Jodo Shinshu shared fully in its peacetime activities, so they shared in the responsibilities when conflict loomed. Every man, woman and child became involved. All hands were needed, and the experience of a century of war taught them that if they lost to a samurai army then the massacre of every member of the community would follow.

In 1575 Oda Nobunaga swept through Echizen Province to recapture it from the local Ikko-*ikki* forces. By November he could boast that he had

Women's corpses appear within the palisade of Hara Castle during the Shimabara Rebellion of 1638. This is clear evidence that women took part in combat alongside their menfolk when the situation was desperate. This is a section from a modern copy of the Shimabara Screen, the original of which is in Akizuki.

In this section from a copy of the Shimabara Screen we see women performing a supportive function while the men of the garrison fight. Wives and daughters bring water in wooden buckets and supply boiled rice from a huge vat.

'wiped out several tens of thousands of the villainous rabble in Echizen and Kaga'. In *Shinchokoki*, the contemporary biography of Oda Nobunaga, his biographer reports: 'From the 15th to the 19th of the eighth month, the lists drawn up for Nobunaga recorded that more than 12,500 people were captured and presented by the various units. Nobunaga gave orders to his pages to execute the prisoners, and Nobunaga's troops took countless men and women with them to their respective home provinces. The number of executed prisoners must have been around 30,000 to 40,000.'

A similar desperate defensive effort is seen a century later in the defence of Hara Castle, which was the culmination of the Shimabara Rebellion of 1637–38. After terrible suffering inflicted by the local *daimyo* the people of the Shimabara Peninsula formed an *ikki* and raised a revolt. In this case the religious ties that bound them together were Christian not Buddhist, but their determination echoed that of the Ikko-*ikki*. When the government forces crushed this rebellion, women and children fought beside their menfolk, wielding pots and pans. On a contemporary painted screen of the siege of Hara Castle there are numerous details showing female involvement in the defence of the castle.

The Shimabara Rebellion was the last uprising to challenge the authority of the Tokugawa family, who had revived the shogunate in their own name in 1603 and ruled until 1868. Few disturbances ruffled the iron rule of the Tokugawa, but when they finally succumbed to the events that marked the transition to modern Japan women warriors fought in the last samurai wars, thus bringing to a close eight centuries of female involvement in Japanese warfare.

APPEARANCE, EQUIPMENT AND DRESS

The armed woman

The woodblock prints used for several illustrations in this work date from many centuries later than the warrior women they represent. There is therefore a tendency to glamorize the appearance of the female samurai, so she is usually depicted in the finest armour of the classical *yoroi* style. This inflexible box-like suit of armour was popular during the Gempei Wars. The samurai woman is also usually left bareheaded or at least un-helmeted so that her delicate female features may be better appreciated. Large *hakama* (wide trousers like a divided skirt) may appear under her armour rather than a tighter-fitting costume to reinforce the fact that she is a woman. Yet in this the artists have done little more than follow written accounts that may themselves have relied on stock phrases and stock descriptions. In reality it is more than likely that a samurai woman defending a castle in 1600, for example, would be dressed in a contemporary style of armour that reflected the changes in defensive costume that had come about in response to developments in weaponry. There was now more danger from bullets than from arrows, so strong breastplates with smooth reflecting surfaces, close-fitting helmets and face masks were the costume of choice.

The *kakemono* (hanging scroll) shown here of Komatsu-dono (1573–1620), the daughter of Honda Tadakatsu and the wife of Sanada Nobuyuki presents several features of a stylized female warrior. As the loyal wife of a retainer of the Tokugawa and the defender of Numata Castle in 1600, Komatsu-dono is shown wearing armour underneath a *jinbaori* (surcoat) that is embroidered with large Tokugawa family *mon* (badge). On her breastplate appears the six-coins motif of the Sanada family. This is likely to have been picked out in lacquer, suggesting that it may be a more modern style of body-armour, and she is also wearing contemporary *haidate* (thigh guards). Other features, however, reflect the fashions of the 12th century when the right arm was left unarmoured to allow freer movement for archery. She also wears bearskin shoes, again a fashion of the time of the Gempei Wars. Her femininity is however emphasized by the voluminous *hakama* under her armour and her long black hair tied back with a white headband. Komatsu-dono, active at the time of the battle of Sekigahara in 1600, has therefore been painted as if she were Tomoe Gozen in 1184. Interestingly, this same anachronistic style was to be deployed by a modern artist in his sketch of the defence of Ueda Castle for the historical novel *Sanada Taiheiki*, even though the samurai shown fighting on either side of her are armed with guns.

There is however one very important contemporary pictorial source from the 14th century that may provide a uniquely authentic appearance of a warrior woman. This is the *Boki ekotoba*, a picture scroll of 1351, which appears in the accompanying illustration. Written

Komatsu-dono, active at the time of the battle of Sekigahara in 1600, appears on this hanging scroll as if she were Tomoe Gozen from the 12th century. The right arm is left un-armoured to allow freer movement for archery and she also wears bearskin shoes, again a fashion of the time of the Gempei Wars. Her femininity is emphasized by the voluminous *hakama* under her armour and her long black hair tied back with a white headband.

ABOVE

With arrows protruding from her armour and her *naginata* under her arm, Tomoe Gozen glances back towards her companion Kiso Yoshinaka as she leaves the battlefield.

ABOVE RIGHT

In this modern book illustration from *Sanada Taiheiki* Komatsu-dono is shown in traditional costume rather than in the armour of the early 17th century, even though the samurai fighting on either side of her are armed with guns. (Reproduced by courtesy of the Ikenami Shotaro Sanada Taiheiki Museum, Ueda).

by Jishun (1295–1360) and illustrated by Kakunyo (1270–1351) this scroll, which is owned by the Nishi-Honganji in Kyoto, contains exquisite and detailed pictures of contemporary life. In the section shown here a wandering *biwa* player is shown entertaining three inhabitants of a warrior monks' temple. All are armoured and two have the monk's shaven heads, but the figure on the left appears to be female. She is kneeling and wearing full armour. In her right hand she grasps the shaft of a bow, while a *naginata* lies across her lap with its blade protruding from the window. It is possible that the figure is meant to represent a youth, but her features are very feminine with rouged cheeks and painted eyebrows, and by comparison the faces of all the other characters are coarse and masculine. The likely conclusion is that she was a wife or daughter of one of the *sohei* (warrior priests) who is fully armed ready for battle. Just as in the case of the 16th-century community-based *ikki*, all the inhabitants of an armed temple had to be prepared to fight when necessary.

The *naginata*

The samurai woman in *Boki ekotoba* is armed with a *naginata*, the traditional weapon for the female warrior, and along with the bow the *naginata* is the weapon most frequently mentioned as being carried by a woman samurai. It is also the weapon usually credited to Tomoe Gozen in pictures of her, although the account of her last battle given below from *Heike monogatari* stresses her accomplishments with bow and sword. In her final fight she also decapitates a samurai, which would have been done with a *tanto* (dagger) rather than a *naginata*.

The *naginata* in the *Boki ekotoba* lies casually in the woman's lap, and so common are the references to *naginata* in the descriptions of women fighting during the Sengoku Period that we must regard a preference for its use as authentic. Certainly by the Tokugawa Period the martial art of *naginata* was a common pursuit for women of the samurai class. The women's *naginata* may then have been lighter in weight than the usual weapon, and practice weapons, like practice swords, were made of wood, but *naginata* was not just a form of physical exercise, as shown by its use during the Boshin War of 1868. In these remarkable accounts, detailed below, the *naginata* is wielded by women warriors as a real and deadly weapon.

In appearance the *naginata* (a word often translated as glaive or halberd) is like a cross between a sword and a spear with a curved blade rather than a straight one. The major difference between a *naginata* shaft and a spear shaft is that the *naginata* shaft is of oval cross section so that it may be more easily wielded for cutting rather than thrusting. The curved blade invariably ended in a very sharp point, but it was the considerable momentum of its cutting edge, delivered with the power of the turning shaft behind it, that made the *naginata* into a formidable weapon. The quality of forging required for the blade of a *naginata* was in no way inferior to that of a sword, and many famous swordsmiths produced celebrated *naginata* blades of varying lengths.

Naginata appear prominently on all the painted scrolls of battles that date from the 13th century and earlier. In these illustrations, however, they are not shown being used by women. Instead it is the weapon of the lower-class warrior. The aristocratic samurai ride horses and carry bows in their roles as mounted archers who display proficiency in *kyuba no michi* ('the way of horse and bow'). Beside them walk small groups of armoured men, some with helmets others without, whose features are deliberately painted to make them look less refined than their betters. Their main weapon is almost always a *naginata* having a large and broad blade akin to Chinese halberds or a blade that is quite long in comparison with its shaft. Later developments of the

The *naginata* was the traditional weapon for a woman warrior. This example, which has a short blade on a long shaft, has a groove running along the length of the blade. It was made around 1615.

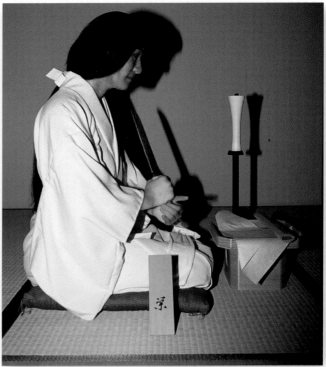

naginata produced a shorter-bladed weapon that was better balanced, and this is the type we usually encounter in pictures of samurai women. The heavier bladed *naginata* was called a *shobuzukuri naginata*. With a sharp blade at one end and a heavy iron ferrule at the other the *naginata* was a formidable weapon in skilled hands. It could be wielded from the saddle or on foot and allowed a range of fighting techniques that was not possible with a straight-bladed spear.

The dagger

Accounts of women using swords are very rare. Tomoe Gozen used a small-bladed edged weapon to decapitate her opponent at the battle of Awazu in 1184. This is likely to have been a *tanto* (dagger), which with its small *tsuba* (guard) resembled a miniature sword, but there were several other varieties of dagger. Acts of suicide by women were likely to be performed using a dagger to the throat, and when it came to offensive weapons the traditional female costume allowed many possibilities for concealing weapons such as small narrow-bladed knives. Inazu Nitobe, using the colourful language typical of his *Bushido; the Soul of Japan* describes their use:

> Girls, when they reached womanhood, were presented with dirks (*kaiken*, pocket poniards) which might be directed to the bosom of their assailants, or, if advisable, to their own…. Her own weapon was always in her bosom. It was a disgrace for her not to know the proper way in which she had to perpetrate self-destruction. For example, little as she was taught in anatomy, she must know the exact spot to cut in her throat; she must know how to tie her lower limbs together with a belt so that, whatever the agonies of death might be, her corpse be found in utmost modesty with the limbs properly composed.

THE SAMURAI WOMAN IN PEACE AND WAR

Wives, daughters and marriage

There is no space here to go into detail about the considerable changes in marriage status, marital location and property rights that took place over the centuries covered by this book. But whatever the overall situation the most cynical use to which a woman of the samurai class could be put remained that of a pawn in a marriage contract arranged for political reasons. In some cases a daughter or a sister might be married off to a known enemy in a desperate attempt to secure peace, making her little more than a hostage, although in many cases the resultant match provided the opportunity for a display of immense loyalty.

The classic examples of political marriages are the experiences of Oichi, the sister of Oda Nobunaga, and her three daughters. Nobunaga was a consummate player of the marriage game, and long before marrying off his sister had involved himself in such a deal when he married the daughter of Saito Dosan (1494–1556), whose territory he coveted. In a cynical move Nobunaga told his wife, quite falsely, that he was plotting with her father's chief retainers to murder him so that Nobunaga could take over. Having been placed in a nice dilemma of loyalty his wife eventually decided to pass on the information to her father Dosan, who obligingly did away with several of his most loyal and innocent retainers. Nobunaga was then able to prevail against the severely weakened family.

By the mid-1560s Nobunaga had full control of the Saito's former territory of Mino Province, and this brought him into armed conflict with Asai Nagamasa (1545–73) from the castle of Odani in neighbouring Omi Province. Peace was secured by sending Nobunaga's sister Oichi to be Nagamasa's wife. This act strengthened Nobunaga's position and enabled him to take the momentous step of entering Kyoto and placing his own nominee in the position of shogun. An early test of Nobunaga's control came when he invited neighbouring *daimyo* to visit Kyoto to pay their respects to the new shogun. Asakura

This statue of Oichi and her family stands in Nagahama, which lies within what was once Omi Province, the territory of Asai Nagamasa, Oichi's first husband. Married to him as part of a political deal by her brother Oda Nobunaga, Oichi faced a dilemma of loyalty when Nagamasa turned against his brother-in-law. When Odani Castle fell Nagamasa committed suicide, but Oichi and her three daughters were spared.

Oichi's second husband was Shibata Katsuie. Once again the match was a political one, but Oichi stayed loyal to her husband until death, and these effigies of the couple are in the Saikoji in Fukui.

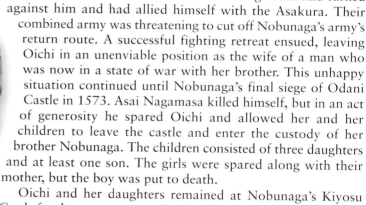

This statue of Oichi stands on the site of Kita-no-sho Castle, where she and her husband Shibata Katsuie perished in 1583.

Yoshikage (1533–73), lord of Echizen Province to the north of Kyoto, refused to attend, an act that gave Nobunaga the pretext for a campaign against him. At first the advance into Echizen went well, but then Nobunaga received the alarming news that his brother-in-law Asai Nagamasa had turned against him and had allied himself with the Asakura. Their combined army was threatening to cut off Nobunaga's army's return route. A successful fighting retreat ensued, leaving Oichi in an unenviable position as the wife of a man who was now in a state of war with her brother. This unhappy situation continued until Nobunaga's final siege of Odani Castle in 1573. Asai Nagamasa killed himself, but in an act of generosity he spared Oichi and allowed her and her children to leave the castle and enter the custody of her brother Nobunaga. The children consisted of three daughters and at least one son. The girls were spared along with their mother, but the boy was put to death.

Oichi and her daughters remained at Nobunaga's Kiyosu Castle for the next ten years. During this time two of Nobunaga's leading generals benefited from the destruction of the Asakura and Asai families. Shibata Katsuie received Echizen and Kaga provinces and established himself at Kita-no-sho (modern Fukui) while Toyotomi Hideyoshi became lord of Omi. When Oda Nobunaga was assassinated in 1582 the two became rivals, each taking the part of a different surviving son of Nobunaga. Shibata Katsuie had been Nobunaga's chief retainer so, anxious to secure Katsuie's loyalty for his own cause, one of the two Oda sons arranged for Katsuie to marry the widowed Oichi.

In 1583 the rivalry between Shibata Katsuie and Toyotomi Hideyoshi developed into bitter warfare with the Shizugatake campaign. Oichi was present with her husband Katsuie in

The three daughters of Oichi went on to become loyal and influential wives. Here we see the three girls engaged in *naginata* practice under the approving if sorrowful eyes of their mother. (From *Ehon Toyotomi kunkoki*, illustrated by Kuniyoshi.)

Kita-no-sho Castle when Hideyoshi besieged it. This time there was no deal with a victorious general, although her three daughters were again sent away to safety Oichi died along with her husband in the burning castle.

The three girls, spared twice from death while watching the destruction of their homes and families, went on to become wives themselves, and each was to make an outstanding and influential contribution to her husband's cause. The eldest, who had the childhood name of Chacha, was to become known as Yodo-dono (The Lady of Yodo'). She became the favourite concubine of Toyotomi Hideyoshi and the mother of his heir Hideyori. Hideyoshi, of course, had brought about the deaths of Yodo's mother and stepfather and been involved in the earlier campaign that had killed her real father, so it appears to be a surprising match. Nevertheless, Yodo proved to be a tower of strength to her son during his minority, staying with him inside his later father's great fortress of Osaka. When Tokugawa Ieyasu laid siege to Osaka in 1614 his European cannon, deliberately targeted onto the apartments used by Yodo, succeeded in dropping a cannon ball onto the tea cabinet she was using at the time. A few days later another shot struck her apartments. This time the cannon ball took out a wooden pillar, which crushed two of her ladies-in-waiting to death. The fear created in Yodo helped to bring the Toyotomi side to the negotiation table. The result was a spurious and deceitful peace treaty that served only to weaken the garrison and its defences. The Tokugawa army returned in the summer of 1615, and once again Yodo did what she could to assist her son, even to the extent of dressing in armour and mounting the battlements. When the final assault was launched Hideyori and his mother sought refuge in the keep, to which the flames had not yet spread, but a senior councillor removed them to a fireproof storehouse. From there Senhime, Hideyori's wife, left under armed protection to seek sanctuary with her father Tokugawa Hidetada, but Yodo stayed behind. A loyal samurai may have put an end to her, although it is more likely that this proud lady took her own life in a way that befitted the consort of the great Hideyoshi.

Oichi's second daughter, Ohatsu, married Kyogoku Takatsugu (1560–1609). As Takatsugu was a Tokugawa man Ohatsu was able to act as a negotiator between the Tokugawa and the Toyotomi sides. She failed to

In this simple but dramatic print Yodo-dono, the mother of Hideyori, prepares to commit suicide as Osaka Castle falls to the Tokugawa in 1615. It is not known for certain if Yodo met her end in this way, but in view of her pride in her samurai family tradition it is more than likely that she did.

prevent the tragedy of Osaka, but saved the life of Hideyori's daughter, who entered a convent after the siege. The youngest daughter was Oe, who married the second Tokugawa shogun Hidetada and gave birth to the third shogun Tokugawa Iemitsu. The complexity of these marriage arrangements meant that Yodo was defending Osaka Castle along with her daughter-in-law Senhime, whose father Tokugawa Hidetada was besieging them. Hidetada, no doubt, was being loyally supported by his own wife who was Yodo's sister!

Another touching example of loyalty is provided by Gohime, the wife of Ukita Hideie. Here was a man who prospered under Toyotomi Hideyoshi but then chose the losing side at Sekigahara. Instead of being executed Hideie was exiled to the tiny island of Hachijo, but Gohime was not allowed to accompany him so instead renounced the world and became a nun.

It must not be thought that all women were invariably loyal to their husbands to the point of death, because it is possible to identify certain wives who acted against the interests of their new families. This is suggested by the existence of various literary warnings maligning a woman's sincerity. 'She may have borne you seven sons, but never trust a woman'. 'Even when a husband and wife are alone together, he should never forget his dagger'. 'Regard another man's pretty daughter as your enemy and never visit her house,' was taking it even further.

Women could also meet horrible deaths when they were manipulated for political ends. When Akechi Mitsuhide besieged Hatano Hideharu's castle of Yakami on behalf of Oda Nobunaga in 1574 he promised to spare Hideharu's life if he surrendered. As earnest of his intentions Mitsuhide gave his own mother to Hideharu as a hostage. She was well treated, but when the surrender was agreed Oda Nobunaga overruled Mitsuhide's wishes and had Hideharu crucified. Even though this was not of Akechi

B **YODO-DONO, THE MOTHER OF TOYOTOMI HIDEYORI, SUFFERS THE BOMBARDMENT OF OSAKA CASTLE, 1614**

Yodo-dono, 'Lady Yodo' was the favourite concubine of Toyotomi Hideyoshi who bore his son and heir Hideyori. When Hideyori was dispossessed following the battle of Sekigahara in 1600 and the establishment of the Tokugawa Shogunate, Yodo began a long campaign to restore his rightful inheritance that culminated in both of them being confined within the walls of mighty Osaka Castle in 1614 by the besieging forces of the Tokugawa. In a psychological ploy designed deliberately to cause terror and to force Yodo to the negotiation table the Tokugawa gunners targeted her apartments, and this scene shows the second occasion when she came under fire. A cannon ball has struck the room, smashing through the wall and taking out a wooden pillar. It has crushed to death two of her ladies-in-waiting. Yodo is dressed in simple white robes that cover all but her face. She and her terrified servants wear beautiful robes that are now spattered with blood within the scene of carnage. Food and broken furniture litter the floor. The scene is set not in the castle keep but inside the *yashiki* (mansion) that lay within the courtyard of Osaka Castle. The keep would provide a refuge only when the final attack came.

In the presence of their *daimyo*, Miyagino and Shinobu attack the swordsman who murdered their father. One has a sickle and chain ready to catch his sword, while the other will finish him off with her *naginata*.

misdemeanour and hid in a paddy field in a village near Shiroishi in Mutsu province. By chance, a farmer, Yomosaku, who had been transplanting rice seedlings, observed him and in his surprise Shiga Daishichi panicked and killed the farmer. Yomosaku had two daughters, the eldest of whom, Miyagino, had (according to the more romantic versions of the tale) been engaged to be married, but through poverty had been sold into prostitution and become a courtesan of the highest status in Yoshiwara, in Edo. The younger daughter, Shinobu, intending to tell her elder sister about her father's death, went to Edo, where she tracked down her sister. They then secretly slipped away from Yoshiwara in order to seek revenge for their father's death, and began to study the martial arts under the guidance of Miyagino's samurai fiancé. They were eager in their pursuit of knowledge, and the result was the vengeance on their father's enemy, Shiga Daishichi, in 1649.

The girls were determined to carry out the revenge themselves, and the details are largely historical. When the time was ripe, they went through the formalities of asking their *daimyo* for authorization to avenge the death of their father. There was, in this case, no need for a long search for the enemy, as he had remained in the *daimyo*'s service. The lord accordingly ordered the man to be brought before him to face the girls in combat. Miyagino was armed with a *naginata* while Shinobu wielded a *kusari gama*, the sharpened sickle to which was attached a long weighted chain. Shiga Daishichi's sword was rendered ineffectual with the aid of the chain, and the other sister finished him off with her *naginata*.

Samurai women and the defended castle

The later sections that describe actual fighting within castles by certain individual women need to be compared with what was normally regarded as the accepted role for a woman to play during the siege of a castle, which included casting bullets, care of the wounded and the preparation of enemy heads for the head-viewing ceremony. These tasks are illustrated by a rare eyewitness account that was recorded by the daughter of a samurai who lived in a castle during a siege. The young girl, later known as Oan, was the daughter of the samurai Yamada Kiyoreki. She describes the siege of Ogaki

This charming life-sized diorama in the Buke-Yashiki at Aizu-Wakamatsu shows a *daimyo*'s wife and daughters at home inside the family mansion. The girls are playing with embroidered balls.

Castle in Mino Province at the time of the battle of Sekigahara in 1600. This was one of the operations whereby the two sides tried to secure as many castles as possible along the main communication routes. Oan begins with effects of the cannon fire:

> When our cannon were to be fired, notice was sent round to all within the precincts of the castle, the reason being that the report of the cannon terrified everyone by shaking the turrets, and seeming almost to make the ground split in two, so that the less courageous – such as the women – should faint right off, and for that reason notice was given beforehand. So when notice had been given and the flash had come, you felt as if waiting for a clap of thunder to follow, and in the early times we all felt as if we should die, and as if there were nothing but fear and horror left. But by and by we saw that it was all nothing…

She and the other women cast bullets in the keep until they were interrupted by requests for assistance with a very different task:

> … our soldiers would bring to us in the turret the heads they had taken, and make us label them for reference. They would also often ask us to blacken the teeth with powder, the reason being, you see, that in the old days 'tooth powder heads' were those of men of rank, and therefore more prized, so that a soldier would bring you a plain head and ask to do him a good turn by giving the teeth a rub of powder. We weren't a bit afraid of the heads, and used to sleep in the midst of the nasty smell of blood that came from them.

Another woman of the samurai class who experienced a siege and lived to tell the tale was Okiku, the daughter of Yamaguchi Mozaemon, who was a lady-in-waiting to Toyotomi Hideyori's mother Yodo. Okiku was present within Osaka Castle at the time of the great siege of 1615. She was then 20 years old, and experienced the shock of seeing bullets hitting the kitchen tables. One tore the edge of a *tatami* (straw mat) and killed a maid. Okiku picked up one of the bullets in her palm, yet she was so confident that Osaka would not fall that later on, when she heard her maid shouting 'Fire!' she assumed that the girl was referring to the noodles she was cooking. But the maid had spotted flames coming out of the Tamatsukuri Gate of the castle. When the fire spread to the huge *yashiki* (mansion) that provided the reception rooms and living quarters in the castle courtyard below the keep, Okiku knew that she would have to evacuate the place. She put on three layers of clothing and paused only to collect a mirror that Toyotomi Hideyori had once given her. Wounded soldiers called out for help as she passed. On escaping from the castle she met up with other women with whom she shared her extra kimono.

The wife of a besieged *daimyo* would support her husband in any way that she could, sometimes coming very close to taking part in the fighting. When Sasa Narimasa attacked Suemori Castle in 1584 Okamura Sukie'mon was ably assisted by his wife in its defence. She walked the walls and inspired the men until Maeda Toshiie rode to its relief. The author of *Taikoki*, the biography of Toyotomi Hideyoshi, was touched both by her martial example and her enduring femininity:

> Okumura's wife was normally meek and generally reserved, a woman with all the elegance such as one would associate with a branch of green willow. However, this heroic court lady who was said to surpass even Lord Nobunaga's own dear mother, accompanied by two or three other persons, armed herself with a *naginata* and day and night without distinction patrolled the castle, and severely warned any soldiers of the guard who were exhausted by the fighting and had fallen asleep.

When a castle fell the consequences for women could be terrible. In 1497 Hojo Soun attacked Fukane Castle and took over a thousand heads. The woodblock-printed edition of the *Hojo godaiki* from which the accompanying illustration is taken shows the heads displayed along the walls. Some are clearly those of women, and more were to suffer at the hands of the Hojo in 1536 when the castle of Sakasai was attacked. The head of the family, Sakasai Muneshige was killed in the fighting, and his wife, the 19-year-old Tomohime, decided to follow her husband in death. She therefore took the bronze bell from the castle that was used for signalling, an heirloom that had been in the family for generations, and slipped it over her shoulders. She then jumped into the castle's moat, and the weight of the bell held her under the water until she drowned.

In this illustration from a woodblock-printed edition of *Hojo godaiki* we see the aftermath of Hojo Soun's capture of Fukane Castle. Among the line of heads placed along the castle wall are ones that appear to be female.

The Hojo came on to the receiving end of warfare in 1590 when Toyotomi Hideyoshi advanced against them. Narita Ujinaga, who commanded Oshi Castle in Musashi Province for the Hojo was absent when Oshi came under attack from Ishida Mitsunari as part of a massive operation to neutralize all the Hojo satellite castles prior to a decisive attack being made on Odawara. Like other Hojo castles, many samurai from Oshi's garrison, including its commander, had been withdrawn to Odawara where it was felt that they were most needed. Ishida Mitsunari was therefore surprised when he discovered that a woman was defending Oshi. Kaihime, Narita's wife, took charge of the defence until the castle had to surrender when a diverted river flooded it. Kaihime was spared, but when Hachioji, another of the Hojo castles, fell to Hideyoshi the women of the garrison jumped to their deaths from its towers to avoid being captured. The topography of the mountain on which Hachioji was built allowed the bodies of the suicides and the slaughtered to be channelled down into the ravine where a mountain stream flowed. Here the waters ran with blood, giving rise to several ghostly legends.

Hosokawa Gracia is revered for the fidelity that she showed to her Christian faith in spite of the initial opposition from her husband, and later his disgrace and death. This statue stands on the site of their castle of Shoryuji near Kyoto.

In 1580 Miki Castle in Harima Province fell to Toyotomi Hideyoshi after a two-year siege. Hideyoshi had wished to spare its commander Bessho Nagaharu (1558–80) and tried to persuade him to surrender peacefully and join Nobunaga's growing band of vassals, but Nagaharu was resolved to fight to the death. His wife Terukohime was equally determined to join him, and when the castle fell the wives and other women of the garrison followed her example in a mass act of self-immolation. In one celebrated case the religious beliefs of the wife of a *daimyo* prevented her from committing suicide. This was Hosokawa Gracia, the staunchly Christian wife of Hosokawa Yusai.

The steps taken to avoid such disasters could be as awful as the situation they were designed to prevent, because sometimes death could not be avoided, only disgrace. In *Ou Eikei Gunki* we read that at the fall of Yuzawa Castle in 1595: 'The castellan Magoshichiro first of all killed his wife and children, the retainers stabbed to death their wives and children as a sacrifice, they set fire to the castle and again fought fiercely in the enemy's midst. Ultimately they threw off their helmets and committed *seppuku*.'

C **THE SUICIDE OF SAKASAI TOMOHIME AT SAKASAI CASTLE, 1536**

When a castle fell, the fate of the women of the garrison could be particularly tragic. Rape, enslavement and even massacres were all not unknown. Here we see the wife of the commander of Sakasai Castle avoiding her fate at the hands of the Hojo in 1536 by committing suicide in a very unusual fashion. Using a long-bladed *naginata* she has cut the rope of the bronze bell that was used for signalling, allowing it to fall over her shoulders. She now staggers forward to the edge of the pond in the courtyard where she will drown herself under the bell's weight. All around lie the bodies of the dead samurai, while to the rear the victorious Hojo samurai are beginning to scale the walls and gain entry. To prepare for her suicide Tomohime has dressed in her finest kimono, and she now sways at the edge of the moat, trying to gauge her position. The bell is based on the actual bell that was used for signalling by the government troops during the Shimabara Rebellion. It is of similar design to a normal temple bell but is much smaller. The castle site is that of the actual Sakasai Castle, recently excavated. Contemporary buildings have been reconstructed in the courtyard.

While spent arrows festoon the outer wooden walls of Hara Castle, the bodies of women lie just within the defences.

THE SAMURAI WOMAN ON THE BATTLEFIELD

Tomoe Gozen: the beautiful samurai, 1184

Tomoe Gozen, the archetypal samurai woman warrior from the Gempei Wars, was the female companion of Minamoto Kiso Yoshinaka, the cousin of the future shogun Minamoto Yoritomo, although her relationship to Yoshinaka is by no means clear. One textual variation of the *Heike monogatari* introduces her as an attendant or servant. The version translated by Sadler, used below, has her down as a 'beautiful girl', from which speculation has added references to her as Yoshinaka's mistress or even his 'warrior wife', but it is fascinating to note that the chapter of *Heike monogatari* that contains the Tomoe story begins by telling us that Yoshinaka had brought with him from his native Shinano province not just one 'beautiful girl' but two. The other's name was Yamabuki, but she had fallen sick and had stayed behind in Kyoto, making Tomoe's exploits unique.

The account of Tomoe Gozen fighting at the battle of Awazu in 1184 in *Heike monogatari* is so brief that it can easily be recounted in full as follows:

> Tomoe had long black hair and a fair complexion, and her face was very lovely; moreover she was a fearless rider, whom neither the fiercest horse nor the roughest ground could dismay, and so dexterously did she handle sword and bow that she was a match for a thousand warriors, and fit to meet either god or devil. Many times she had taken the field, armed at all points, and won matchless renown in encounters with the bravest captains, and so in this last fight, when all the others had been slain or fled, among the last seven there rode Tomoe.

After describing Yoshinaka's final manoeuvres the account returns to Tomoe Gozen:

But now they were reduced to but five survivors, and among these Tomoe still held her place. Calling her to him Kiso said, 'As you are a woman, it were better that you now make your escape. I have made up my mind to die, either by the hand of the enemy or by mine own, and how would Yoshinaka be shamed if in his last fight he died with a woman?' Even at these strong words, however, Tomoe would not forsake him, but still feeling full of fight she replies, 'Ah, for some bold warrior to match with, that Kiso might see how fine a death I can die!' And she drew aside her horse and waited. Presently Onda no Hachiro Moroshige of Musashi, a strong and valiant samurai, came riding up with 30 followers, and Tomoe, immediately dashing into them, flung herself upon Onda and grappling with him, dragged him from his horse, pressed him calmly against the pommel of her saddle and cut off his head. Then stripping off her armour she fled away to the Eastern Provinces.

The archetypal samurai woman Tomoe Gozen is shown here on horseback, wielding her *naginata* to great effect. Samurai are being knocked off their feet by her charge. Tomoe is shown bare-headed to contrast her femininity with her fury.

That is the last we hear of her in *Heike monogatari*, although *Gempei seisuki* tells us more, adding that Yoshinaka expressly directed her to take the story of his final battle back to his home province of Shinano. But before leaving the field she was attacked by Wada Yoshimori, one of Yoritomo's chief retainers, using a pine trunk as a club. She twisted the trunk in her hands and broke it into splinters, but Wada Yoshimori caught her and made her his concubine. She was to bear him a son, the celebrated strong man Asahina Saburo Yoshihide who was killed in 1213 when the Hojo family destroyed the Wada family. Tomoe then became a nun and lived to the age of 91.

This modern print of Tomoe Gozen shows her cutting off the head of Onda Moroshige at the battle of Awazu in 1184, an incident related in *Heike monogatari*.

Tsuruhime of Omishima, the sea princess, 1541

On the island of Omishima in the Inland Sea stands an important Shinto establishment called the Oyamazumi Shrine. It is famous for its collection of arms and armour donated over the centuries as votive offerings by famous samurai who offered prayers to the guardian *kami* of Oyamazumi before going into battle. Among the suits of armour on display is one of an unusual shape with a tapered waist. It was clearly made for a woman, and according to a very strong local tradition was worn in battle by Tsuruhime, the daughter of the shrine's chief priest, whose claim to divine inspiration coupled with fighting skills has led to her being compared with Joan of Arc.

Tsuruhime was born in 1526. At that time the island was under threat from the growing power of Ouchi Yoshitaka (1507–51) from Yamaguchi on the mainland of Honshu, and fighting took place between the Ouchi and the Kono family of Iyo Province on Shikoku Island, under whose jurisdiction the shrine fell. Tsuruhime's two elder brothers were killed in one such conflict, and when Tsuruhime was 16 years old her father died of illness, so she inherited the position of chief priest. She had been trained since childhood in the martial arts, and when the Ouchi made further moves against Omishima she took charge of the military resistance. Proclaiming that she was not merely the inheritor of the shrine's guardianship but the avatar of the Mishima Myojin (the shrine's powerful *kami*), she led an army into battle and drove the Ouchi samurai back into the open sea when they raided Omishima in 1541.

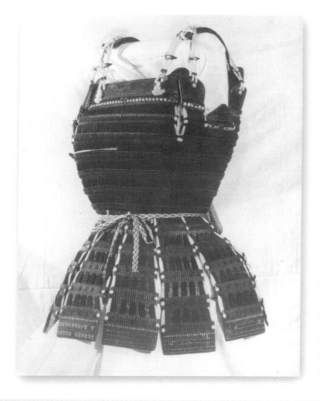

This suit of armour, clearly made to fit the contours of a woman's body, is on display within the treasure house of the Oyamazumi Shrine on the island of Omishima, and is associated with the female samurai Tsuruhime.

D **TSURUHIME TAKES PART IN NAVAL FIGHTING, 1541**

Tsuruhime, the daughter of the chief priest of the Oyamazumi Shrine on Omishima in the Inland Sea is the 'Joan of Arc' of samurai history. Believing herself to be the avatar of the shrine's *kami* (deity) Tsuruhime took charge of the island's defence against Ouchi Yoshitaka's expansionist policies. In this plate we see Tsuruhime, dressed in the armour attributed to her that is still preserved in the Oyamazumi Shrine treasure house, engaged in single combat with Obara Nakatsukasa no jo, the commander of the Ouchi army in 1541. Obara has been sitting in state on the deck of his flagship enjoying a cup of sake and has been surprised both by the unexpected attack and by the fact that a woman is leading it. Exploding bombs flung from Tsuruhime's ship begin to burst around them. The *horokubiya* (spherical bombs) are thrown by hand by *ashigaru* (foot soldiers) from the deck of Tsuruhime's ship. The bombs with burning time fuses are being whirled round the head. Tsuruhime is dressed following the usual artistic convention for pictures of her. Her armour from the shrine is the only protection she has, thus emphasizing her femininity and the divine protection she believed was hers. Tsuruhime's armour is a very simple *haramaki*, fastening at the back, which is laced with dark blue cords. She is carrying a sword rather than a *naginata* for convenience in sea fighting. Her companions are more conventionally dressed, but their armour is deliberately lighter for ease in sea fighting. Their victim, with a haughty disregard for his safety, is wearing an elaborate and heavy *do-maru* armour of a style popular during the mid-16th century. The ship is based on scale models of the *ataka-bune* type in Osaka Castle Museum and the Pirates Museum on Oshima. The flags of the Ouchi and of the Ohori (Tsuruhime's priestly family) are shown.

Four months later the invaders returned, and while the Ouchi general Obara Nakatsukasa no jo was being entertained on his flagship he came under attack from Tsuruhime in a raid. Using a 'bear paw' rake she climbed on board and sought out the general for single combat. At first he mocked her presumption, but Tsuruhime cut him down. This was followed by a deluge of *horokubiya* (spherical exploding bombs) from Tsuruhime's allies, which drove the Ouchi fleet away. Two years later, at the age of 18, she was again in action against an attack by the Ouchi, but when her fiancé was killed in action she committed suicide by drowning.

Ueno Tsuruhime at Tsuneyama, 1577

The modern traveller crossing from Honshu to Shikoku across the Seto–Ohashi Bridge can see in the distance on the Okayama prefecture side the site of the castle of Tsuneyama. Thirty-four graves stand in one section of the castle hill. They are the graves of the members of a remarkable unit of female samurai warriors.

Tsuneyama Castle was owned by the Mimura family of Bitchu Province, who became engulfed in the major military operation conducted on Nobunaga's behalf by Toyotomi Hideyoshi between 1577 and 1582 along the San'yodo Road, the highway that followed the coast of the Inland Sea. The objective was to control the powerful Mori family and their numerous allies, some of whom proved willing to submit peacefully to Nobunaga. Others, such as Bessho

Tsuruhime's statue stands within the ground of the Oyamazumi Shrine on Omishima, which the 'Joan of Arc of Japan' defended so valiantly against the forces of Ouchi Yoshitaka.

The *naginata* developed from a fierce polearm to a weapon regarded as suitable for women to exercise with. In this picture a servant girl of Oda Nobunaga uses it for its original purpose during the attack on the Honnoji temple in 1582 that led to Nobunaga's death. (From *Ehon Toyotomi kunkoki*, illustrated by Kuniyoshi.)

In Kiyosu Castle a life-sized diorama shows Oda Nobunaga performing an extract from a Noh play. Beside him sits this servant girl playing a drum.

Nagaharu, whose wife's suicide at Miki Castle was described earlier, put up a stronger resistance.

The Mimura family were among those who joined Nobunaga's side early on in the campaign, and this put their castle of Tsuneyama in peril. A certain woman of the Mimura named Tsuruhime (not to be confused with the other Tsuruhime of Omishima) was married to Ueno Takanori, a staunch ally. When Tsuneyama came under attack by the Mori army it seemed likely that defeat would be rapid, so it was decided that the mothers and daughters of the Mimura should commit suicide one by one followed by their lord. Tsuruhime's husband also was resolved to die, so she immediately decided that if she was going to die it would not be at her own hand, and prepared to lead a sortie out of the castle to die in battle. We are told that Tsuruhime donned a suit of armour, took in her hands a *naginata* with a 'white shaft' (which may indicate plain wood) and thrust a *wakizashi* (short sword) through her belt. She then went down into the castle courtyard and invited the other women of the garrison to join her. They were very reluctant to do so because they believed that women who fought in battle would be punished in the afterlife. Tsuruhime assured them of the reverse, that they should not fear death because death on the battlefield would lead to the Western Paradise of Amida Buddha in the Pure Land. At this the castle gate was opened and Tsuruhime led a suicidal charge into the midst of the enemy, accompanied by 33 other women whom she had inspired. The first reaction from the Mori samurai was one of surprise and disbelief, but then Tsuruhime caught sight of a man who appeared to be the enemy general and attempted to challenge him to single combat. The challenge was not accepted, and, unlike the case of the other Tsuruhime, the guards provided no opportunity for her to act alone, and none of the other besieging samurai seemed prepared to kill a woman. Frustrated in her desire to die in battle, Tsuruhime ordered her fighting women to withdraw to the castle. There they recited the *nembutsu* (the act of calling on the name of Amida Buddha), took hold of their swords and killed themselves by flinging their bodies forward onto the sharp blades.

Keigin-ni at Imayama, 1570

The battle of Imayama in 1570 provides a case study of a woman acting indirectly to bring about a victory. Otomo Chikasada had laid siege to Ryuzoji Takanobu's castle of Saga. Saga had a garrison of only 5,000 men against Otomo's probable 60,000, who were spread in a huge arc round Saga, anchored at each end on the sea coast. Scouts, however, brought news that Otomo Chikasada was planning to hold some form of celebration inside his field headquarters that night, prior to attacking Saga the following morning. The base was located on the hill of Imayama, about 6km (4 miles) north-west of Saga castle, and 3,000 of his bodyguard were there with him. To Nabeshima Naoshige, the Ryuzoji's leading retainer, it was an ideal target for a night raid, but most of his colleagues did not agree. It was apparently Ryuzoji Takanobu's mother, Keigin-ni, who shamed them into following Nabeshima's advice with the words, 'Isn't your attitude towards the enemy forces like a mouse in front of a cat? If you are real samurai then carry out Nobushige's night raid on the Otomo headquarters. Decide between life or death and victory or defeat!'

That night a detachment of Ryuzoji samurai and foot-soldiers, keeping their advantage of height, silently approached the curtained area on the lower slopes of Imayama and waited until just before dawn. The Otomo troops had

Hostages were usually well treated unless treachery on the part of the hostage giver was suspected. This illustration shows the latter instance, as Kamei Shinjuro presents to those who have broken their truce the heads of their wives and children. (From *Ehon Toyotomi kunkoki*, illustrated by Kuniyoshi.)

clearly enjoyed their pre-battle party, and were sleeping off the effects of the sake. Even the guards must have been lulled into a false sense of security by their own overwhelming numbers, because without any warning being given Nabeshima Naoshige ordered his harquebusiers to open fire, and 800 samurai charged down into the position. They first extinguished all the Otomo's pine torches that provided the only night-time illumination, and then began to extinguish the Otomo samurai. Otomo Chikasada was cut down, and 2,000 of his *hatamoto* (guards) were also killed. Taking advantage of the confusion, Ryuzoji Takanobu led another attack out of the castle against a different section of the siege lines. So devastating was the night raid that the Otomo withdrew the rest of their troops.

Myorin-ni, the warrior widow of Tsurusaki Castle, 1586

Myorin-ni is the posthumous name that appears on the *ihai* (funerary tablet) of one of the best-authenticated and most remarkable examples of a woman taking on an actual fighting role in a battle. Once again the context is that of a defended castle where a woman was to be found left in charge but, unlike other examples where the husband was absent because of military duties considered to be more important, Myorin-ni was the keeper of the castle in her own right following the death of her husband eight years earlier.

Myorin-ni was the widow of Yoshioka Kamon-no-suke Shigeoki, a senior retainer of Otomo Sorin Yoshishige (1530–87), the *daimyo* of Bungo Province (modern Oita Prefecture) on Kyushu. Otomo Yoshishige lived at a time when the influence of European traders and missionaries was at its height, and he embraced European trade, culture, weapons and (ultimately) its religion with an enthusiasm that was unparalleled among his contemporaries. In 1562 Yoshishige left the administration of his main castle of Funai (in modern Oita City) to his son and made a new headquarters for himself in the castle of Usuki on the little island of Nuijima. It was at this point that he shaved his head and became a Buddhist monk under the name of Sorin, and it is as Otomo Sorin that this future Christian *daimyo* is best known. With his ego and his arsenal continually boosted by his European connections Sorin pursued an expansionist policy until the limits of Otomo territory collided with the similarly expansive borders of the mighty Shimazu of Satsuma Province. In 1578, the same year that Otomo Sorin finally accepted Christian baptism, the two sides met in battle at Mimigawa, a disaster for the Otomo that left three of their generals dead and thousands of their samurai strewn along the riverbank like autumn leaves.

Among the dead at Mimigawa lay the 30-year-old Yoshioka Shigeoki, the keeper of Tsurusaki Castle that lay between two rivers a little to the east of Funai. His son Yoshioka Munemasu was only ten years old, and so great had been the swathes cut into the Otomo leadership that there was no alternative but to leave Tsurusaki Castle for the meantime in the capable hands of Shigeoki's widow Myorin-ni. Over the next few years Myorin-ni did indeed prove to be highly capable in the peacetime administration of the castle while Otomo Sorin consolidated his position now that any hopes of expansion had been curtailed.

In 1586 Myorin-ni's role changed dramatically to that of having to defend Tsurusaki Castle against an attack. Bolstered by their victory over Ryuzoji Takanobu at the battle of Okita-Nawate in 1584 the Shimazu of Satsuma moved against the Otomo in 1586, concentrating their attacks upon the three fortresses of Funai, Tsurusaki and Usuki. The defences of Usuki, which lay on sheer cliffs connected to the mainland by a sandbar, included a Portuguese breech-loading

近江國粟津が
原にて木曽義
仲ぞ木曽義
仲能弱義経
合戦度々の敵の
大軍主に佐はふ
義仲敗軍ふ
ならびに今井
四郎兼平勇
戦えて死の図

巴御前

和田右門義盛

In this small detail from a print of the battle of Awazu in 1184 Tomoe Gozen is shown wielding her *naginata* in a single combat with a mounted samurai swordsman.

cannon called 'kunikuzushi' (the destroyer of provinces), which was being used to defend a fortress for the first time. It was mounted near the main gate on a stone platform that allowed a clear field of fire over the narrow stretch of sea and on to the dry land beyond. The Shimazu were shaken by the novelty of the bombardment, but regained their composure sufficiently to mount an assault. This was beaten off, and soon the operation deteriorated into a stalemate.

The siege of Tsurusaki, which was not defended by cannon, proved to be a very different affair involving hand-held firearms and bows and arrows. The army of 3,000 men was led by the three Shimazu generals who expressed surprise on discovering that a woman was defending the castle. Myorin-ni appeared on the walls dressed in full armour and carrying a *naginata*, but the numerous Satsuma casualties produced by the firearms wielded from within the castle soon made them realize that here was a serious enemy. Negotiations were set in motion and Myorin-ni was offered substantial reward in gold and silver if she would surrender the castle, but she made it clear that she was prepared to defend it to the death.

Time was of the essence because Toyotomi Hideyoshi had now joined the fight against the Shimazu, and he was preparing to invade Kyushu, ostensibly to help the Otomo. The defence of Tsurusaki under Myorin-ni was kept up with vigour, the garrison losing only one man during the main assault and taking 63 heads of the Satsuma attackers. The heads were forwarded to Otomo Sorin in Usuki, who was much encouraged thereby. The heroic Myorin-ni was clearly in the thick of the fighting because during one assault she sustained a deep arrow wound and was captured. The Shimazu general Nomura treated her with the greatest respect and took her to the castle of Takashiro. Ironically this was the castle where a siege in 1578 had led to the battle of Mimigawa and the death of Myorin-ni's husband. She did not recover from the wound, and died there in the same place as her husband. But Myorin-ni's action at Tsurusaki had bought time for Hideyoshi, and the great invasion of Kyushu that encompassed the defeat of the Shimazu was facilitated by her action, one of the finest operations to be led by a woman.

The women of Hondo, 1589–90

When the minor landowners of the Amakusa Islands rebelled against the incomer Konishi Yukinaga in 1589 he and Kato Kiyomasa led an expedition against the castles of Shiki and Hondo. The resistance by a largely Christian *ikki* was fierce, and involved action by women as recorded by the Portuguese Jesuit Luis Frois, who may have been physically present in Hondo. Led by the wife of the castle commander and the wives of his senior retainers, 300 women, many of whom had husbands who had been either killed or wounded, made their confessions to the priests and resigned themselves to death in battle: 'in order to fight freely and without any hindrance, as a group they cut off their hair, and so that their long kimonos would not get in the way they discreetly tied up the hems. Certain of them put on armour, others wore swords at their belts, others too had spears, still others had various weapons about their persons, and in addition to armour they had rosaries and reliquaries hanging round their necks.'

As a body the 300 women sallied out from the broken castle gate and took by surprise the attackers who were stationed in the area immediately adjacent to them:

> One section of the moat was almost filled with the enemy soldiers killed by the women. Yet whatever the immediate outcome may have been, Toranosuke's (Kiyomasa's) soldiers possessed numerical superiority, and even though the women had overcome some male enemy soldiers, they could not tolerate the dishonour of defeat by the surviving women and children, so in a scene that must have been terrifying they responded with a fierce attack, and out of the 300 women there were only two survivors, both of whom were severely wounded. In this way was the entire group of the women put to the sword, and their bodies lay exposed on the battlefield. Later on the enemy soldiers would remark, 'The warriors of Hondo were not men. They were women and children, yet the men who were fighting were surpassed by the dauntless courage of these warriors.'

The female defenders of Omori Castle, 1599

Hideyoshi's conquest of the Shimazu on Kyushu was followed by his subjugation of the mighty Hojo in 1590. This latter achievement so impressed most of the major *daimyo* of Tohoku (north-eastern Japan) that one by one they came to pledge allegiance to him. Some resistance remained, although this was concentrated among small *daimyo* in remote areas, who had fought each other for decades with little regard for political

developments in the rest of Japan. Yet even while these pockets of unrest continued Hideyoshi felt sufficiently confident to set up the 'Taiko Kenchi', a process whereby land use and ownership for the whole of Japan was surveyed, valued, reallocated if necessary and placed under the appropriate control so that it could be converted to a tax yield. By 1598, the year of Hideyoshi's death, almost all of Japan had been surveyed, but there had been fierce resistance in several places where the process had provoked riots and uprisings.

In Tohoku the Onodera family of Dewa Province fought Hideyoshi's representative Otani Yoshitsugu (1559–1600) with great vigour, and in 1599 Onodera Yasumichi was faced with an attack by Yoshitsugu's army against the fortress of Omori, a naturally strong position built at the confluence of two rivers. Local resistance against the land survey had been felt at all social levels, so that it was a heterogeneous *ikki* army of Onodera samurai and farmers that defended Omori against the Otani army. The siege was fought out in the bitter cold of a Tohoku winter, with valuable contributions being made by the women of the garrison. The following extract from *Ou Eikei Gunki* describes their inspired use of makeshift catapults:

Tomoe Gozen, the most famous female warrior of all, is shown here in a very stylized print. She is in full armour with voluminous *hakama* (trousers) worn underneath. She also has a courtier's tall *eboshi* (cap) on her head.

The retainers of Serita, Shiyoshi and Nikaho at the set time rode their horses to the steep side to the west and left them there, then advancing on foot they broke down the palisade and crossed the moat, but at the spot where they were on the point of driving in every single one of the two or three hundred women from within the castle came out and began to throw down an abundance of large and small stones which they had already prepared, shouting as they defended [the castle], whereupon more than 20 men were suddenly hit and died. Many more were wounded. In fact, and regrettably, because of the women's act of opportunity of throwing stones, driven by necessity and scrambling to be first they jumped into the moat and fled outside the palisade. This treatment inspired those within the castle.

E **THE WOMEN OF OMORI DEFEND THEIR CASTLE, 1599**

No women suffered more in warfare than the members of *ikki* (leagues) who defied a *daimyo's* power. Massacres were the norm for a defeated *ikki*, so battles were fierce, particularly those involving sieges. Here we see the resistance led by the Onodera family of Dewa Province against the troops of Otani Yoshitsugu, who was trying to apply the decisions concerning land-holding set out by Toyotomi Hideyoshi. Hundreds flocked to the Onodera standard in what was virtually a 'peasants' revolt' led by samurai. In this scene we see the ingenuity displayed by the women who helped defend Omori Castle against Otani Yoshitsugu. Omori is built on a natural plateau, making it ideal for defence with catapults. These were simple affairs on the Chinese model where the propulsion was by people pulling on ropes. The women, warmly clad against the snow, but otherwise simply dressed as one would expect of the wives of part-time samurai-farmers, operate the catapults while many more throw stones by hand, hurling down a hail of stones onto the advancing samurai. The appearance of Omori Castle is based on the reconstructed Takane Castle.

About 20 harquebuses opened fire. This was not enough to frighten [the women], and the throwing of small stones from the shadows of the moat was like a hailstorm. To the irritation of Shiyoshi, they struck Ishii Ukon Koremichi in both eyes and killed him. Similarly, they struck in one eye the horse that Kutsuzawa Goro was riding with his bow hand but did not kill it. Saying, 'to stay too long in that place and be hit by women's stones would be a failure bringing ridicule for generations to come', they returned to the original point of attack. As for these stones the unequalled strength of the women was unexpected, but Fukusei-ln had skilfully prepared from timber machines for throwing stones. When operated by women and children, they could easily project them about 1 *cho* (120m).

Women in the Sekigahara Campaign, 1600

When Toyotomi Hideyoshi died, the country that he had so recently reunified threatened to break apart again over the right to rule of his infant son Hideyori. Events came to a head within two years at the battle of Sekigahara in 1600, where Ishida Mitsunari and his coalition of pro-Hideyori *daimyo* were defeated by Tokugawa Ieyasu (1542–1616) who became the first Tokugawa shogun in 1603. Decisive though Sekigahara was, its effects could have been nullified by events elsewhere in Japan where supporters of the two sides fought their own battles. Sekigahara is therefore better understood as a campaign lasting several months in four crucial areas of operation. These locations were the area to the east of Kyoto where considerable battles took place for control of the castles along the Tokaido; the strategic fortress of Ueda on the Nakasendo Road; Tohoku and Kyushu. Remarkably, three out of these four theatres provide authentic examples of samurai women warriors.

The Sekigahara campaign began with a complex and confusing series of actions designed to secure a number of castles along the Tokaido and the Nakasendo highways. One of these was Anotsu in Ise Province (modern Tsu in Mie Prefecture). Tomita Nobutaka held it for Ieyasu, and when he was called away to serve the Tokugawa Anotsu came under attack from Ishida Mitsunari's army under Nabeshima Katsushige (1580–1657). As in other similar cases, Tomita's wife Yuki no kata took charge of the situation and defended the castle successfully for the Tokugawa.

The samurai woman who became associated with Ueda Castle was Komatsu-dono (1573–1620), the daughter of Tokugawa Ieyasu's famous retainer Honda Tadakatsu (1548–1610). Ieyasu had adopted her for use in a political marriage and arranged for her to be married into the Sanada family, with whom he had concluded peace after a humiliating failure to capture outright their castle of Ueda in 1586. Sanada Masayuki (1544–1608) the defender of Ueda, sent his eldest son Nobuyuki (1566–1658) as a hostage to the Tokugawa as part of the peace agreement, and it was to Nobuyuki that Komatsu-dono was married. From that time on Sanada Nobuyuki became a staunch Tokugawa supporter in direct opposition to the views of his father and his brother Yukimura. The final split occurred just before Sekigahara. Nobuyuki owned Numata Castle in Kozuke Province, and when Ieyasu issued the call to arms that was to lead to the decisive battle, Nobuyuki followed the Tokugawa while his father and brother espoused the cause of Ishida Mitsunari.

Sanada Nobuyuki left Numata in the hands of his wife Komatsu-dono when he set off to join Ieyasu, only to have Numata surrounded by the army of the other two Sanadas. Komatsu-dono resolutely refused to surrender the castle or even to give admittance to her father-in-law, who claimed that he only wanted to visit his grandchildren! She announced that if the Sanada army tried to force their way in she would burn the castle to the ground and commit suicide. Her defiance paid off and Sanada Masayuki and Yukimura withdrew to Ueda. As they had anticipated, Ieyasu's son and heir Tokugawa Hidetada approached Ueda while on the way to reinforce his father, but instead of masking Ueda with a holding force as had been his orders, he proceeded to lay siege to the fortress. Sanada Nobuyuki was among the besiegers, and as he had with him many Sanada men who had relatives inside the castle he became concerned that this would affect their fighting spirit. In a brilliant move he and Komatsu-dono arranged for all non-combatants such as wives, children and elderly parents to be allowed to leave on humanitarian grounds. They were kindly allowed to enter Numata Castle, where Komatsu-dono confined them virtually

This print shows Komatsu-dono the daughter of Honda Tadakatsu, who was married to Sanada Nobuyuki. She served her husband loyally when she refused entry to Numata Castle to their rivals from within the Sanada family. She is shown with a *naginata*.

49

This simple portrait is on display on the funerary altar of the temple in Yanagawa where Ginchiyo lies buried. Ginchiyo was the warrior nun of Yanagawa who held up the advance by Kato Kiyomasa at her convent in 1600.

as hostages while the siege continued. In the end Tokugawa Hidetada abandoned the siege and hurried along the Nakasendo, but managed to join his father only after the battle of Sekigahara had finished. Ieyasu was so angry that he first refused to see his son, whose dallying could have lost them the battle. Sanada Nobuyuki and his brave wife were rewarded for their part in the action, and Komatsu-dono died in 1620, honoured as a samurai woman who had supported her husband in a very dramatic fashion.

The 'Kyushu Sekigahara Campaign' saw the rivalry between Tokugawa Ieyasu and Ishida Mitsunari being fought out by their supporters in southern Japan. Tachibana Muneshige (1569–1642) the *daimyo* of Yanagawa Castle was a supporter of Ishida Mitsunari and after Sekigahara fled back to Kyushu to seek refuge. Ieyasu sent after him Nabeshima Katsushige, Kuroda Josui and Kato Kiyomasa, and the resulting military action was to provide a unique example of a variation on the familiar theme of warrior monks in the person of Ginchiyo, the warrior nun of Yanagawa.

Tachibana Muneshige had taken no part in the actual battle of Sekigahara, because on the same day as that great defeat for the Ishida cause he had achieved a notable victory by capturing Otsu Castle from Kyogoku Takatsugu. The operation took two days and provided an entertaining spectacle for the local people who, unafraid of the competing armies, had taken picnic boxes to the nearby hills and watched the proceedings. The defeat at Sekigahara made Muneshige's prize meaningless, so he hurried back to Yanagawa. By the time he arrived Tokugawa Ieyasu's main ally on Kyushu, Kuroda Josui Yoshitaka (1546–1604) had taken considerable steps towards controlling the island for the Tokugawa cause. Yanagawa soon came under attack, but its defence was helped by the presence of a small defended strongpoint to the south of his castle in the shape of the convent where Tachibana Muneshige's divorced wife, Ginchiyo, now resided.

GINCHIYO, THE WARRIOR NUN OF YANAGAWA, RECEIVES THE THANKS OF HER EX-HUSBAND TACHIBANA MUNESHIGE, 1600

When Kato Kiyomasa and Nabeshima Katsushige advanced upon Yanagawa Castle in 1600 their way was blocked by a small defended strongpoint to the south of his castle in the shape of the convent where Tachibana Muneshige's divorced wife Ginchiyo now resided as a Buddhist nun. In an act of surprising loyalty to her ex-husband Ginchiyo organized her fellow nuns in armed resistance against the advancing army. Here we see Ginchiyo and Muneshige reunited after the battle, and the campaign finally resulted in the peaceful surrender of Yanagawa and the restoration of the Tachibana to favour with the Tokugawa. Ginchiyo is dressed in the habit of a Buddhist nun. Her head is covered, and over her long deep red-purple robes she wears the Buddhist monk's *kesa* (ceremonial 'apron') and carries a Buddhist 'rosary' in her hand. The grateful Tachibana Muneshige, tired and scarred from battle, is still wearing his characteristic armour with a modern smooth reflecting breastplate, set off with an individual *zunari*-style helmet ornamented with a ring-shaped crest and a plume of black cock's feathers. His *mon* (badge) appears on the back of his *jinbaori* (surcoat).

In an act of surprising loyalty to her ex-husband Ginchiyo organized her fellow nuns in armed resistance against the advancing army of Kato Kiyomasa who was proceeding from the south. It is interesting to note that two of the besiegers of Yanagawa, Kato Kiyomasa and Nabeshima Katsushige, already had experience of fighting against women warriors, which may have accounted for the respect they gave to Ginchiyo's act of defiance.

We know very little about the actual defensive measures adopted by Ginchiyo. Her resistance may have been only one of dressing up in armour and looking defiant, but it seems to have made the point. Kuroda and Kato were old comrades-in-arms of Tachibana Muneshige from the days of the Korean invasion, and following the unexpected resistance by Ginchiyo they proposed that he should surrender and join them in a campaign against the Shimazu, who had also fled from Sekigahara. Muneshige agreed, but Ieyasu ordered the campaign to stop almost before it had begun because he did not want a further war in Kyushu. Tachibana Muneshige was pardoned nonetheless.

The women warriors of Aizu, 1868

The Meiji Restoration of 1868, by which the Tokugawa *bakufu* ended its days in favour of an imperial restoration, was by no means the popular and bloodless revolution it is often supposed to be, and the war provided a remarkable instance of samurai women in action on a battlefield.

In 1868 the Boshin Civil War was fought between the newly established government under young Emperor Meiji and supporters of the ousted shogun. On the imperialist side the chief protagonists were the two *han* (*daimyo* fiefs) of Satsuma and Choshu, while the *han* most loyal to the shogun was Aizu, situated in the north of Japan and as far away from Satsuma and Choshu as it was possible to be both in terms of geography and politics. The Matsudaira family of Aizu were a branch of the Tokugawa. In January 1868 Aizu, and other supporters of the shogun, attempted to recapture Kyoto but were heavily defeated at Toba-Fushimi. The imperial army then marched on Edo, where they captured the ex-shogun without bloodshed. The city was renamed Tokyo (the eastern capital) and became the seat of the new Meiji Government, which quickly found that it could not ignore the sizeable core of pro-Tokugawa support that still existed in northern Japan. The neighbouring *han* of Sendai refused to attack Aizu, so 3,000 government troops arrived in Matsushima Bay to put pressure on the *han*'s rulers. But the heavy-handed treatment of Sendai backfired and provoked instead a loose alliance of northern *han* loyal to the shogun who were determined to resist the imperialists.

The government's strategy was to pick off the northern domains one by one. Their opponents fought bravely, but most surrendered quickly against the better-armed and better-organized imperialist troops. The Meiji Government originally

Although these warriors may at first sight look like young men, they are in fact members of the Joshigun, the name later given to a unit of women formed in Aizu Castle who fought with their *naginata* against the imperial government troops. As a female fighting unit they were following an honourable yet largely unrecognized tradition going back to the 16th century

planned to leave Aizu to the last, but their general Itagaki Taisuke pressed for an immediate attack before the snow started to fall, when soldiers from the warm climes of Satsuma would not fare well in the northern Japanese winter. Among the records of the operation there exists a remarkable account written by a man called Shiba Goro. At the time of the attack on Aizu-Wakamatsu Castle he was only ten years old and so was sent away from the fighting. He later wrote his memoirs, and included details about the battles and the sad fate of his family. He also describes watching his sisters practising with their wooden *naginata* in the garden with white bands tied around their hair and kimono sleeves tucked up. The rumours he was hearing about the war confirmed everyone's feeling that even women might have to fight: '... rumours circulated of troops running wild. According to one rumour, *ronin* (masterless samurai) from Satsuma and Choshu were setting fires and murdering people in Edo and other places to stir up unrest, bringing further dishonour to the Tokugawa and foment hatred of Aizu. According to another rumour, the enemy troops left in their wake the corpses not only of soldiers, but also of innocent townsmen, peasants, women and children.'

Aizu's women were the most authentic women warriors in the whole of Japanese history. They received expert training in the use of *naginata*, and were educated to be proficient in both pen and sword. Their weapons were to be used in the defence of their *han*, their *daimyo* and their families – in that

In this dramatic picture we see the 'apotheosis' of the women of Aizu-Wakamatsu, who committed suicide there in 1868.

order. The advancing government army was soon in possession of a gate in the northern outer wall of Aizu-Wakamatsu Castle. At this point the Aizu leaders rang the fire bell, which was the agreed signal for the elderly men, women and children to seek safety in the castle. They had however been advised by Matsudaira Katamori that, although it was his intention to fight to the death to wipe out the stain on Aizu's honour, the non-combatants were free to act as they wished. One samurai's 14-year-old son wrote afterwards: 'I hastened to the inner enclosure of the castle. I knew of course I would never return home… not that I had the time to think of such matters…. All the women in my family had resolved to die, and yet, as I took leave, not one person shed a tear.'

Many of the non-combatants stayed at home simply because they felt that their presence within the castle would hinder the fighting men and needlessly consume vital food supplies. This was a particularly brave decision in view of the rumours of Satsuma and Choshu samurai slaughtering civilians in Edo. It may be this fear of being killed, rather than the demands of samurai tradition, that led to the remarkable events that followed, because 230 non-combatants are known to have taken their own lives as Aizu-Wakamatsu fell. Young Shiba Goro had been moved to a place of safety, but while he was away his grandmother, mother, oldest brother's wife and two sisters killed themselves. In the family of Saigo Tanomo, a senior Aizu retainer, his mother, wife, five daughters and two sisters killed themselves. Other women in his extended family also committed suicide, making a total of 22 female deaths from this one family. His sisters and daughters even composed farewell poems:

Each time I die and am reborn in the world
I wish to return as a stalwart warrior
These were the words left behind by his older sister. The younger wrote:
I have heard that this is the way of the warrior
And so I set out on the journey to the land of the dead.

NAKANO TAKEKO GOES INTO ACTION AGAINST THE IMPERIAL ARMY, 1868

The involvement by women in the siege of Aizu-Wakamatsu Castle in 1868 provides one of the most remarkable and authentic instances of women warriors in the whole of Japanese history. Motivated by intense loyalty to their pro-shogunate *daimyo*, and with a genuine belief that defeat at the hands of the Satsuma-Choshu forces would mean certain death, women such as Nakano Takeko fought alongside their menfolk and often exceeded them in daring. Nakano Takeko led a sortie by women of the so-called Joshigun unit, who charged into the fire of the imperial army's modern rifles wielding only their *naginata* and swords. When the imperial troops realized that they were facing women the cry went up to take them alive, but holding their fire meant that the women were soon upon them. Nakano Takeko killed five or six men with her *naginata* before being shot dead. Her sister Masako then cut off Takeko's head so that it would not be taken as a trophy, and the severed head was safely taken back to a local temple.

The appearance of Takeko is based upon contemporary descriptions of her and her comrades. Their hair was tied back with a *hachimaki* (headband). A white *tasuki* (sash) held the sleeves of what is effectively the male costume of *haori* (jacket) and *hakama* (trousers), but their weapons remain those of the traditional woman warrior. Through their belts are thrust a *katana* and a *wakizashi* (long and short swords), with most fighting being done using the *naginata*. Their opponents from the imperialist Satsuma army are ordinary infantrymen wearing conical helmets over blue uniforms, although their officer sports an example of the *koguma*, the shaggy 'mane' on his head, the colour black indicating that he is from Satsuma. Their red brocade sleeve tags indicate that they are imperial troops. Their Spencer repeating rifles, the most modern firearms available to either side at Aizu, are of little immediate avail against the sudden fury of the women.

In this picture hanging in the restored Confucian Academy of the Aizu *han* we see women and children of the garrison extinguishing fires started by the bombardment from the imperial troops.

Other women accompanied their menfolk to the castle, where they assisted in the defence and were fully prepared to go into battle themselves. Some of them fought only after they had already dispatched members of their own families in an orgy of assisted suicide, but this was not for some abstract concept of loyalty or samurai honour. They firmly believed in the rumours that the western domain troops would slaughter them all or sell them as slaves. In one extraordinary instance, Kawahara Asako, the wife of the magistrate Zenzaemon, cut off her hair and decapitated her mother-in-law and daughter before seeking death in battle, *naginata* in hand, and drenched in blood. In this she was initially unsuccessful, because she was swept back inside the castle's walls by a wave of retreating Aizu warriors.

The name Joshigun was later to be given to the platoon of up to 30 samurai women who fought alongside the men in the defence of Aizu-Wakamatsu Castle when the imperialists broke in. They cut their waist-long hair to shoulder length and tied it back in the young man's hairstyle. They were armed with *naginata* and swords. One mother and her two daughters joined in a mixed-gender sortie out of the castle, but became caught outside when the defenders barred the gate. They decided to make their way to where other Aizu forces were active. But no sooner had they joined up with their comrades than they came under attack near Yanagi Bridge. Committed to their cause, and determined not to be taken alive, the Joshigun women

charged into the fire of the imperial army's modern rifles, wielding only their *naginata* and swords.

What followed was a bloody encounter that would have been more in keeping with the story of Tomoe Gozen rather than the year 1868. When the imperial troops realized that they were facing women the cry went up to take them alive, but holding their fire meant that the women were soon upon them. Nakano Takeko killed five or six men with her *naginata* before being shot dead. In an another extraordinary echo of a medieval battle her sister Masako then attempted to cut off Takeko's head so that it would not be taken as a trophy. A male comrade helped the exhausted Masako, and the severed head was safely taken back to a local temple. Outgunned and defeated, the survivors, both male and female, eventually made their way back to Aizu-Wakamatsu Castle. The siege lasted thirty days in all. Shiba Goro writes about his conversation with a survivor.

According to Shiro, the women in the castle had played an extremely courageous part in the defence. Whenever a cannon ball landed they ran to the spot and covered it with wet mats and rice sacks before it could explode. They cooked meals and nursed the wounded without respite, heedless of the damage done to their clothes. Bespattered with blood, they had outdone themselves in helping the men. And they had been fully prepared, if necessary to change into their white kimono and charge into the enemy with their *naginata*.

Here we see women of the Aizu-Wakamatsu garrison tending the wounded during the siege of 1868.

Further confirmation of the bravery of the women of Aizu comes from Dr William Willis, a British doctor who accompanied the government troops during the Aizu campaign to help the wounded. On entering the town he treated several hundred of the Aizu wounded, whom he found 'in a deplorable state of filth and wretchedness', and in a memorandum Willis refers to the bravery and energy of the women in the castle, who 'cut off their hair, busied themselves in preparing food, nursing the wounded, and in not a few instances, shouldered the rifle and bore a share in the fatigues of watching'.

The defence continued with night raids being launched on the government positions, and at least one woman took part in them. This was Yamamoto Yaeko (1845–1932), whose father, a gunnery instructor, was killed while defending the castle. Yaeko was competent with modern rifles as well as *naginata*, and began participating in night raids armed with a Spencer rifle and samurai swords. After the defeat of the shogunate forces she moved to Kyoto to look after her brother who was taken prisoner by the Satsuma army and suffered harsh treatment. She became a Christian and eventually married a preacher. Yamamoto Yaeko lived to a ripe old age and helped found Doshisha University in Kyoto. A third woman, Yamakawa Futaba (1844–1909) who participated in the defence also survived and later became involved in the promotion of female education.

Many other women, both fighters and non-combatants, were to perish when General Itagaki launched an all-out offensive on 29 October 1868. His troops burned the samurai houses in the outer castle precincts while 50 cannon pounded the castle day and night, some from as far as over a mile away. The Aizu troops responded with old-fashioned 4-pdr mortars with a range of only 78m (85 yards), but on 6 November, one month after the siege had begun, a white flag was raised above the northern gate. During the nine months between the battle of Toba-Fushimi and the fall of Aizu-Wakamatsu Castle, 2,973 Aizu people had died in action. Two thousand five hundred and fifty-eight were soldiers; 130 were men over the age of sixty; 52 were children; and 233 were women. Some of the women had died from injuries sustained from the artillery bombardment. Others had killed themselves, while a small but proud number had written their own unique chapter in samurai history.

YAMAMOTO YAEKO INSPIRES THE MEN OF THE AIZU GARRISON, 1868
Yamamoto Yaeko (1845–1932) is one of the other celebrated women warriors of Aizu, and her example of bravery and skilled sharpshooting inspired the men of the castle of Aizu-Wakamatsu during the desperate siege by the imperial forces in 1868. Unlike Nakano Takeko, her preferred weapon was not the *naginata* but the Spencer rifle, few of which were available to the pro-shogunate forces of Aizu. Yaeko was however the daughter of a gunnery instructor who was killed while defending the castle, and her father had trained her in the use of modern weapons as well as traditional ones. Like Nakano Takeko, she is shown here dressed in male attire, as recorded by eyewitnesses. Her costume consists of the traditional wear of the samurai, with short pleated *hakama* worn over leggings and straw sandals. Her jacket is tied back with a white sash to leave her arms free for wielding weapons. Around her head she wears a white *hachimaki* (headband). Her appearance thus contrasts with the soldiers of the garrison, who are dressed in similar style to their enemies from Satsuma in the previous plate, but with the variations that distinguished the Aizu *han*, notably the distinctive sleeve badge with the character 'ai' for Aizu. Some wear *hakama* over their dark blue uniforms and on their heads are traditional Japanese 'fore and aft' lacquered straw hats. Unlike Yaeko's Spencer rifle, their simpler weapons are muzzle-loading percussion cap rifles. In the background can be seen one of the huge walls of Aizu-Wakamatsu Castle where an ornamental red bridge crosses the moat.

Some of the Satsuma troops who fought at Aizu would take part a decade later in the last war of the samurai era. This was the Seinan War of 1877, better known in the west as the Satsuma Rebellion. The Satsuma rebels under Saigo Takamori had a few women in their ranks, including Takamori's own daughter Chikako. But this was the last that Japan was to see of samurai women warriors. Just as the elite samurai class gave way to the conscript army of the modernizing Meiji Government, so did women warriors give way to men, and Japan's modern wars, from the Sino-Japanese War to World War II, were all-male affairs.

Saigo Chikako was the daughter of Saigo Takamori, and fought during the Satsuma Rebellion of 1877.

MUSEUMS AND MEMORIALS

As most Japanese museums have a policy of rotating objects in their collections and operate an extensive loans programme it may be possible from time to time to come across certain illustrations or objects associated with samurai women. The permanent collections listed here tend to be small and are owned by the Buddhist temples where the particular historical figure is buried. Perhaps the best example of this is the Shinsho-In, a temple in Hachioji to the west of Tokyo on the Chuo Line. Here is buried Matsuhime, the daughter of Takeda Shingen who was married to Oda Nobunaga's son. An effigy of her as a Buddhist nun appears in the main temple hall and her grave lies in the cemetery to the rear. There is also a small private chapel, not normally open to the public, which contains a striking wooden image of Matsuhime, together with pictures of her and her actual *naginata*. Not far away is the site of Hachioji Castle where certain features have been sensitively rebuilt and one can see the mountain stream that ran red with the blood of the slain garrison and their families.

The wives of the Sato brothers are richly remembered in the vicinity of Shiroishi in Miyagi Prefecture. The Kacchudo in Shiroishi contains life-sized wooden images of the pair, while more modern effigies of them are on display in the main hall of the Ioji Temple in Iizaka. Here there is also an excellent museum with several scroll paintings of the women.

A historical drama for television several years ago brought the story of Tsuruhime, the 'sea princess' of Omishima to the attention of a wide audience, and in the Oyamazumi Shrine on the island, which has long been the repository for one of the finest and most important collections of weapons and armour in all Japan, Tsuruhime's suit of armour, tailored for a female body, is on show. Two modern statues of her stand in the shrine precincts.

Oichi, Oda Nobunaga's unfortunate sister, is commemorated in Nagahama through her connection with her first husband Asai Nagamasa, and more particularly in the city of Fukui, where wooden images of her and her second husband Shibata Katsuie are displayed in the small museum in the compound of the Saikoji Temple. Statues of the couple also appear on the site of Katsuie's castle of Kita-no-sho in Fukui. Oichi's second daughter is buried in a temple in Obama, the fief of her husband Kyogoku Takatsugu, in Fukui Prefecture. Hosokawa Gracia is remembered at the rebuilt Shoryuji Castle in Nagaoka

In the Shinsho-In in Hachioji, where Matsuhime, the daughter of Takeda Shingen, is buried, her *naginata* is preserved in a private chapel.

This modern statue, preserved behind glass in the main hall of the Ioji temple in Iizaka, is of Wakazakura, one of the wives of the two Sato brothers.

The grave stone in the middle marks the grave of Ginchiyo, the warrior nun of Yanagawa, in her funerary temple in Yanagawa.

to the south of Kyoto. Her grave is in the Koto-In, which is one of the sub-temples of the Daitokuji complex in Kyoto. Strangely, there is no memorial to Yuki no kata in the partially rebuilt castle of Anotsu in the city of Tsu in Mie Prefecture. Ginchiyo, the warrior-nun of Yanagawa, lies buried in a temple in Yanagawa. Komatsu-dono is similarly honoured in a temple in Ueda, but only a marker on the site of her castle of Tsurusaki remembers Myorini-ni in Oita.

The city of Aizu-Wakamatsu takes pride in and derives much profit from its association with some of the fiercest battles of the war of 1868, but most of the emphasis is on the male defenders of the castle, particularly the youthful 'White Tigers' who committed mass suicide on a nearby mountain. There is a statue to Nakano Takeko complete with *naginata*, and there are pictures of the Joshigun in the rebuilt castle.

The revenge of the sisters Miyagino and Shinobu is remembered in two locations in Shiroishi in Miyagi Prefecture. The first is a small commemorative pavilion on a hillside, while their weapons are preserved in the Senneji Temple, although they are not on show to the public. The temple also owns a comprehensive collection of woodblock prints relating to the incident.

BIBLIOGRAPHY AND FURTHER READING

Ackroyd, Joyce, 'Women in Feudal Japan' in *Transactions of the Japan Society of London* (1957) pp. 31–68

Akasegawa, Jun et al., *Himegimitachi no dai sengoku emaki* (Tokyo, 2009)

Akita, Kaishinhosha (ed.), *Kosenjo: Akita no kassen shi* (Akita, 1981)

Aston, W. G., *Nihongi* (Reprint) (North Clarendon, VT, 1972)

Birt, Michael P., *Warring States: A Study of the Go-Hojo Daimyo and Domain 1491–1591* (Unpublished PhD Thesis, Princeton, 1983)

Chamberlain, Basil Hall, 'A Short Memoir from the Seventeenth century: Mistress Oan's narrative' in *Transactions of the Asiatic Society of Japan* (1881) pp. 37–40

Conlan, Thomas, *State of War: The Violent Order of Fourteenth Century Japan* (Ann Arbor, 2003)

Inagaki, Shisho, 'Onna no katakiuchi' in *O-ie sodo to katakiuchi* (*Raibaru Gekitotsu Nihon shi Vol. 6*) (Tokyo, 1979)

Kuwada, Tadachika (ed.), *Shinchokoki* (Tokyo, 1966)

Matsuno, Tsuneyoshi *Wives of the Samurai* (New York, 1989)

Matsuoka, Hisato (ed.), *Nambokucho ibun, Chugoku, Shikoku hen* (Tokyo 1987–95)

McCullough, Helen Craig, *The Taiheiki* (New York, 1959)

——, 'The Tale of Mutsu' in *Harvard Journal of Asiatic Studies* (1964) pp. 178–211.

Nagaoka, Kyonosuke, 'Appare! Kojo no kaikyo' in *O-ie sodo to katakiuchi* (*Raibaru Gekitotsu Nihon shi Vol. 6*) (Tokyo, 1979) pp. 66–69

Sadler, A. L. 'Heike Monogatari' *Transactions of the Asiatic Society of Japan* 49 (1921)

Sakasai Board of Education, *Sakasai-jo* (Sakasai, no date)

Sasama, Yoshihiko, *Buke Senjin Saho Shusei* (Tokyo, 1968)

Shiba, Goro, *Remembering Aizu: The Testament of Shiba Goro* (Honolulu, 1999)

Tabata, Yasuko, *Nihon chusei no josei* (Tokyo, 1987)

——, *Nihon chusei no shaki to josei* (Tokyo, 1998)

Takeuchi, Rizo (ed.), *Kamakura ibun* (Tokyo, 1971–97)

Togo, Ryu, *Onna katchu roku* (Tokyo, 2006)

Tsunoda, R. et al., *Sources of Japanese Tradition Vol. 1* (New York, 1958)

Wright, Diana E., 'Female Combatants and Japan's Meiji Restoration: the case of Aizu' *War in History* 8 (2001) pp. 396–417

Yokoyama, Shigehiko, *Kassenjo no onnatachi* (Tokyo, 2010)

Yoshida, Yutaka (ed.), *Taikoki Vol. 1* (Tokyo, 1979)

INDEX

Figures in **bold** refer to illustrations.

Henry VIII's dissolution of the monasteries in 1536-39 also contributed to the problem. The monasteries had not only provided much direct or indirect employment, but had also been a significant source of alms to those in need. Such factors contributed to a substantial increase in the number of unemployed men roaming around the country in search of work and, if they could not find it, turning to vagrancy and begging.

Various parliamentary Acts were passed during the 1500s which aimed to curb begging and also to place on local parishes the responsibility for providing relief to the deserving or 'impotent' poor – those who could not work due to old age, sickness etc. An Act of 1536 required churchwardens to collect voluntary alms both to relieve the poor, sick and needy, and to set to work 'sturdy and idle vagabonds and valiant beggars'. Begging was always treated as a serious offence and in 1547 the Statute of Legal Settlement enacted that a sturdy beggar could be branded or made a slave for two years (or for life if he absconded). The same Act condemned any 'foolish pity and mercy' for vagrants, but for the impotent poor it proposed that cottages were to be erected for their habitation, and that they should be relieved or cured. In 1563, the contributions to parish funds by householders for poor relief became compulsory rather than voluntary. A further Act in 1576 stipulated that every town should set up stocks of materials (wool, flax, hemp, iron etc.) for the unemployed able-bodied poor to work on, either in their own homes or in a workshop. Every county was also to set up a punitive House of Correction for dealing with any able-bodied pauper who refused to work.

THE OLD POOR LAW

Elements from these earlier statutes were brought together in 1597 in an Act for the Relief of the Poor, re-enacted in a slightly revised form in 1601. The 1601 Act, the cornerstone of what became known as the Old Poor Law, laid down that the parish was the body responsible for poor relief, and that relief was to be funded by the local poor rate raised from householders. Materials were to be bought to set the able-bodied poor to work (with the threat of the House of Correction for anyone refusing to do so), while 'houses of dwelling' could be set up for the impotent poor.

The poor rate was collected by a parish official called an overseer (an unpaid and often unpopular post) and administered by the parish Vestry (a committee comprising the minister, churchwardens and a number of householders). Most parish poor relief was distributed as 'out-relief' – handouts in the form of money, food, fuel and clothing, to people living in their own homes.

Although the 1601 Act talked about 'work' and 'houses', it did not mention 'workhouses' – establishments which provided accommodation for the poor and where work had to be performed by those inmates who were able to do so.

EARLY WORKHOUSES

The earliest workhouses, such as one set up in York in 1567, were more like what we would now call workshops, that is, non-residential establishments where raw materials such as wool, hemp, flax or iron were supplied to provide work and training to the poor. At Sheffield, the Corporation's accounts from 1628 onwards record that they spent around £200 on the erection of a workhouse together with a stock of raw materials for providing employment. Eight shillings was spent on 'the carpenters' charges going to Newarke to see their workhouse'. Another early establishment was in Halifax, which in 1635 was granted a charter by Charles to set up a workhouse. Gradually, the idea evolved of providing the poor with both work and lodging in a single establishment, often with the former being required in return for the latter.

Although the words workhouse and poorhouse are often used interchangeably, the term poorhouse can sometimes denote an establishment, often for the elderly, where work was not required and a kinder regime operated, for example where there was no resident Master and no prescribed diet. Another point of terminology of particular relevance to the north of England concerns the term 'parish'. Northern parishes often covered a large area within which several centres of population, or 'townships', were located. From 1662, such townships were put on a par with parishes for the purposes of poor relief.

SETTLEMENT

The 1662 Settlement Act spelled out who a parish or township was responsible for – namely, those who could claim 'settlement' there. A child's settlement at birth was taken to be the same as that of its father. At marriage, a woman took on the same settlement as her husband. Illegitimate children were granted settlement in the place they were born – this often led parish overseers to try and get rid of an unmarried pregnant woman before the child was born, for example by transporting her to another parish just before the birth, or by paying a man from another parish to marry her.

Settlement could also be acquired in various ways, for example by renting a property for at least £10 a year, but this was well beyond the means of an average labourer. If a boy became apprenticed, which could happen from the age of seven, his parish of settlement became the place of his apprenticeship. Another means of qualifying for settlement in a new parish was by being in continuous employment for at least a year. To prevent this, hirings were often for a period of 364 days rather than a full year. On the other hand, labourers might quit their jobs before a year was up in order to avoid being trapped in a disagreeable parish.

CIVIC INCORPORATIONS

In 1696, Bristol promoted its own local Act of Parliament enabling it to set up a corporation for the management of poor relief, including the establishment of a workhouse. More than thirty large towns eventually went down this path beginning in 1698 with Colchester, Crediton, Exeter, Hereford, Shaftesbury, Tiverton, and – one of the few northern towns to be so incorporated – Kingston-upon-Hull.

Hull's Corporation workhouse, located on Whitefriargate, was known as Charity Hall. The Corporation comprised the town's Mayor, Recorder, twelve Aldermen, and twenty-four other inhabitants. However, the initial scheme was apparently not a success and the workhouse proved 'almost useless', being used instead for the next thirty years as a training school and home for pauper children. Early urban workhouses often targeted pauper children as a group likely to be in need of care, but who could be usefully trained and perform work to contribute towards their maintenance.

THE WORKHOUSE TEST

The early 1700s saw a growing use of the workhouse by parishes to try and limit the growing demand on the poor rate. This was achieved in two ways. First of all, placing paupers together in a single house could in itself save money compared with providing food, heating and rent for a large number of people in their own homes. Second, a parish could decide to make the workhouse the only form of relief it was prepared to offer in the hope that this would deter spurious claims. Anyone who was prepared to suffer entry into the workhouse could be judged worthy of sufficient need. In 1723, this so-called 'workhouse test' became incorporated into Knatchbull's Act which provided a clearer framework for parishes to set up and operate a workhouse.

Knatchbull's Act also allowed parishes to contract-out the time-consuming business of running a workhouse, a procedure which became known as 'farming' the poor. The contractor